Poland's Struggle

Poland's Struggle

Before, During and After the Second World War

Andrew Rawson

Pen & Sword
MILITARY
AN IMPRINT OF PEN & SWORD BOOKS LTD.
YORKSHIRE – PHILADELPHIA

First published in Great Britain in 2019 by
Pen & Sword Military
An imprint of
Pen & Sword Books Ltd
Yorkshire – Philadelphia

ISBN 978 1 52674 392 3

A CIP catalogue record for this book is
available from the British Library.

Printed and bound in the UK by TJ International Ltd, Padstow, Cornwall.

Pen & Sword Books Limited incorporates the imprints of Atlas, Archaeology,
Aviation, Discovery, Family History, Fiction, History, Maritime, Military, Military
Classics, Politics, Select, Transport, True Crime, Air World, Frontline Publishing,
Leo Cooper, Remember When, Seaforth Publishing, The Praetorian Press,
Wharncliffe Local History, Wharncliffe Transport, Wharncliffe True Crime and
White Owl.

For a complete list of Pen & Sword titles please contact

PEN & SWORD BOOKS LIMITED
47 Church Street, Barnsley, South Yorkshire, S70 2AS, England
E-mail: enquiries@pen-and-sword.co.uk
Website: www.pen-and-sword.co.uk

Or
PEN AND SWORD BOOKS
1950 Lawrence Rd, Havertown, PA 19083, USA
E-mail: Uspen-and-sword@casematepublishers.com
Website: www.penandswordbooks.com

Contents

Introduction

If you search for books on Nazi Germany, you will be inundated with titles covering the pre-war rise of the National Socialists. There are also hundreds of titles covering their military campaigns and genocidal activities across Europe. The same goes for the Holocaust, with many titles on the ghettos, deportations and extermination camps involved in the destruction of Europe's Jews. However, there are very few titles on the Polish experience in the twentieth century.

The centenary of the re-creation of the Polish State was celebrated on 11 November 2018, a date more commonly associated with the end of the First World War. It is also the date chosen to remember those who died in both world wars around the world. But it means something else in Poland: it is the nation's birthday. The same goes for 1 August, the date the Warsaw Uprising began in 1944. The streets of the city come to a standstill as the sirens sound. Then red flares are lit as the crowds stand in silence to remember those who fought and died challenging the Nazis and the Soviets, in an attempt to regain the nation's independence. Their families did get their freedom, but only after forty-five years of communist rule, which involved political terror, hard labour and food shortages.

I became interested in the history of twentieth century Poland as a result of two separate experiences. In 2013, I visited Kraków on a research trip for two guide books. The first covered the story of the infamous Auschwitz-Birkenau Death Camp, which is 100 kilometres south-west of the city. However, it was the second one which opened my eyes to the suffering endured by the Polish people during the Second World War. It covered Kraków's story, and while I initially thought it would primarily be about the events surrounding Oskar Schindler and the *Schindler's List* story, it was clear there was far more to it than that.

I was well aware of the Jewish Holocaust which had been largely conducted on Polish soil by the Nazis, but my research introduced me to many stories I knew only a little about: the invasion of Poland and the extermination of the Polish intelligentsia; then there was the suppression of the rest of the Catholic Poles, including slave labour, interrogations and executions; there were heroic tales of the underground forces, involving such groups as the Armed Victory Struggle, the Home Army and the Grey Ranks; the story culminated with the Red Army advances in early 1945, resulting in communist oppression which lasted for many years.

Over time, I have met several Poles who have expressed an interest in my books about military history. Most had an interesting family story to tell about World War II, as well as their own experiences of communism. They also asked me what I knew about Poland's history during the Second World War and I had to admit I knew little more than the basics we find on the television or in news articles. So I began digging, and found, as I said at the beginning, that books are few and far between except for one subject: the Jewish Holocaust.

The result of my research is this book. It is not a comprehensive history of twentieth-century Poland, but it goes far beyond the usual narratives currently available. It starts with the re-creation of a nation after over 100 years under the yoke of three large empires. It then moves through the difficult stabilisation of a nation under threat from all sides, particularly after the Nazis seized power in Germany. The military campaign of 1939 is followed by the suppression of the nation and its people by the Nazis and the Soviets before they go to war. There are stories of mass executions, brave uprisings and fighting back from overseas, because one thing was certain, the Poles were never going to give up until their country was free. The story ends with a summary of forty-five years of communism which ultimately breaks down to make way for a free and democratic nation.

Learning about Poland's experiences has greatly increased my knowledge of Eastern Europe in the past and it has given me an interesting insight into how that part of the world feels about its history today. I hope this book does the same for you.

Andrew Rawson, November 2018

The new nation of Poland after the battles with its neighbours following the First World War.

Chapter 1

Poland is Not Yet Lost

Establishing an independent state, 1918 to 1933

The First World War

The German and Austro–Hungarian Empires asked the ethnic Poles to fight the 'Muscovite Yoke' when war broke out in August 1914. Meanwhile, Tsarist Russia owned three-quarters of ethnic Poland and half a million Poles answered Grand Duke Nicholas's appeal to join the Russian army, after he promised to give them their independence. What they did not know was that the tsar secretly planned to take control of the area as soon as his armies had defeated the Germans and Austro-Hungarians.

The area the Polish coveted was captured by the German and Austrian armies in the summer of 1915. They soon agreed to give the Russian area to the Poles while splitting the rest of ethnic Polish territory between them. A compromise peace between Russia, Germany and Austria late in 1916 complicated matters but the plan to create a Polish nation out of the Russian areas remained. They would not be given sovereignty but they could form an independent army. An agreement was signed by Kaiser Wilhelm and Emperor Franz Joseph in December, and while the Poles were happy, everyone else protested.

Every Pole hoped for independence but some wanted to stage a revolution to get better terms. Józef Piłsudski commanded the Polish Legions in the Austrian Army but he was encouraging his men to join the secret Polish Military Organisation. He was convinced the Central Powers would lose the war and he resigned from his post in the summer of 1916. Piłsudski refused to give in to Austria's demands to swear an oath to the Empire the following spring and so he and the Legion officers were arrested, while their men were drafted.

The United States President, Woodrow Wilson, called for a 'united, independent and autonomous Poland' in his 'Peace without Victory' speech on 22 January 1917. Everything changed a few weeks later because the Romanov dynasty collapsed, the United States entered the war, and the

Austro-Hungarian Empire became unstable. But the tables turned again when the Kerensky offensive failed in July 1917 and Russia's future looked uncertain.

As the events on the Eastern Front unfolded, the Polish community in North America formed their own army to serve on the Western Front, hoping to increase the chance of creating an independent Poland. Over 20,000 Poles were trained and shipped to France in the spring of 1917, where they received French arms and equipment. Many women joined the Polish Central Relief Committee at the same time to support the war effort.

The French President, Raymond Poincaré, and the Polish statesman, Ignacy Paderewski, signed the alliance which brought the Polish army into existence on 4 June 1917. It became known as the Blue Army because the troops were given the French army horizon blue uniforms. They were joined by another 35,000 Poles who had served in the French army or who had been captured while serving in the Axis armies. They were all organised under French military control and were commanded by General Louis Archinard.

The Bolsheviks seized power across the Russian Empire on 7 November 1917, and they accepted that the Poles had a right to independence, so the Polish Regency Council established a cabinet. On 8 January 1918, President Wilson promised an 'independent Polish state' in his 'Fourteen Points'. The ending of hostilities on the Eastern Front with the signing of the Treaty of Brest-Litovsk the following March 1918 also worked in the Poles' favour.

But there was still plenty of fighting to be done. Polish troops were first engaged in combat on the Western Front in July 1918 and they fought throughout the autumn campaigns. General Józef Haller von Hallenburg would take command of the Blue Army on 4 October 1918. Despite their contribution on the Western Front, members of the Blue Army were never recognised as war veterans by either America or Poland. It meant that Polish–Americans would refuse to help future Polish military causes.

Deciding the Borders

The Regency Council had demanded Polish independence but it was a rival council headed by Piłsudski which took control of the new state on 11 November 1918. The day is remembered as the day Poland gained its independence.

All German troops were made to leave the new state before the parliamentary (known as *Sejm*) elections were held at the end of January. The Supreme Council recognised the Polish government a month later, but its borders still had to be set. The Poles decided to set their own, by fighting the Lithuanians and Ukrainians; they then had to defend themselves against the Bolsheviks.

Roman Dmowski suggested that Poland's Second Republic could be made the same size as the First Republic, with alterations to suit current circumstances. However, that would make Poland too big and French Prime Minister Georges Clemenceau, British Prime Minister David Lloyd George and President Woodrow Wilson, each argued their case. France wanted an alliance with Poland as security against Germany, while Britain wanted a balance of power across Europe. Meanwhile America believed an ethnically pure Poland would form the strongest nation.

After long discussions, Poland received parts of Germany, including parts of West Prussia, East Prussia, Silesia and Poznań. It included the area known as the Polish Corridor, giving access to the Baltic Sea. But the port of Danzig was made a free city under the League of Nations' control, so the Poles started building their own sea port: Gdynia. No one was really satisfied when the Council broke up at the end of June and Poland's eastern border still had to be sorted, because Russia was in turmoil.

Dealing with Neighbours

The new nation of Poland may have regained its independence after 123 years but it faced difficult times with its neighbours, while the Treaty of Versailles argued over its borders. It had to assert itself against Germany, Lithuania and the Ukraine before coming under attack from the Soviet Union.

Seizing German Territory

A rousing speech by Ignacy Paderewski had resulted in the start of the Greater Poland Uprising across the Poznań district on 27 December 1918. Germany was powerless because it was in a state of revolution and the area was given to Poland under the terms of the Treaty of Versailles. The Polish Corridor was transferred at the same time, connecting Poland to the Baltic Sea.

The shooting of Silesian civilians by German border guards in August 1919 resulted in strikes and German troops being deployed. Hundreds of Poles were executed and many more escaped into Poland to escape the violence, until British and French troops restored order. A German newspaper then falsely announced that the Red Army had captured Warsaw in August 1920, resulting in pro–German marches and riots, so the Poles countered by taking control of Silesia (*Śląskie* in Polish).

Arguments over the spring 1921 referendum results resulted in more trouble and Allied troops again had to quell the violence. Upper Silesia's industrial region and its one million citizens (mainly Germans) were finally handed over in October 1921, making it Poland's powerhouse.

Tens of thousands of ethnic Germans left Poland during these turbulent times, some to find work and some to escape discrimination. But others were deported because they refused to become Polish citizens. Many left when the Soviets invaded in the summer of 1920, either to avoid conscription or because they feared a Bolshevik victory. Altogether around 800,000 ethnic Germans had left the western regions of Poland by 1923.

Annexing Lithuania

The Lithuanians had claimed Vilna (now Vilnius) as their capital and announced a new Republic of Lithuania on 2 November 1918. The government escaped to Kaunas when the Red Army entered the city two months later, but the Poles drove the Bolsheviks out in April 1919. Piłsudski (who was Lithuanian) wanted to reunite the two peoples but the Lithuanians wanted their independence. A Polish coup failed to oust the Lithuanian government in August 1919 and so Piłsudski signed the Treaty of Warsaw with Ukrainian leader Symon Petliura the following April.

The Lithuanians initially joined the Poles in the war with the Bolsheviks in July 1920, only to occupy the territory they wanted and sign a peace treaty with the Soviets. However, the Poles defeated the Bolsheviks in August and then turned on the Lithuanians. The League of Nations ended the conflict with the Suwałki Agreement on 7 October 1920, but the Lithuanians still controlled Vilnius.

Polish soldiers immediately seized the city, on the pretext of protecting the Polish community, and while their actions were condemned as a mutiny, they had been organised by Piłsudski. General Lucjan Żeligowski responded by declaring a new Republic of Central Lithuania. A referendum in January 1922 was a Polish victory (although the results had been rigged). It meant that Poland could annex the Vilna area while the new border was agreed at the Entente Council of Ambassadors (the successor of the wartime Supreme War Council) in March 1923. The Lithuanians still maintained their claim on their historic capital and they would refuse to enter diplomatic relations with Poland until 1938.

Fighting the Ukrainians

The Ukrainians had seized Kiev and declared themselves a republic back in November 1917 before announcing their independence from Russia in January 1918. The Bolsheviks recaptured Kiev in February 1918, so the Ukrainians sent food to Germany, in return for military support. They were then able to retake Kiev and the conflict ended with the Treaty of Brest-Litovsk.

The Bolsheviks annulled the treaty when the First World War ended, and there were fresh disturbances in East Galicia. Fighting escalated over the winter until a cease-fire was agreed in the spring. However, the Bolsheviks took advantage of the situation to incorporate the central and eastern territories into the Ukrainian Soviet Socialist Republic.

The Allies had supported the Poles because they thought they would stop the Bolsheviks advancing across Western Europe, but they attacked the Ukrainians, who wanted their independence, instead. Their victory helped to set Poland's borders, which were decided by the League of Nations in October 1921.

As already mentioned, despite their contribution on the Western Front, the members of the Blue Army were not recognised as veterans by either America or Poland. It meant that Polish-Americans would refuse to help future Polish military causes.

Haller's 35,000 strong Blue Army was transported across a restless Germany in sealed trains with their weapons locked away because of the ongoing revolution. The Allies thought they would be deployed to stop the Bolsheviks but they attacked the Ukrainians instead. Poles had the advantage but there was another stalemate in July 1919. Piłsudski agreed to turn on the Bolsheviks in April 1920 in return for control of Eastern Galicia. But the Bolsheviks won and they secured their Republic before driving the Polish army back towards Warsaw. The Entente Council of Ambassadors eventually agreed that Poland could keep Eastern Galicia and the annexation was made formal on 15 March 1923.

Facing the Soviet Onslaught

Russia's ruling Council of People's Commissars had initially recognised Poland's right 'to decide its own fate and to become reunited' on 29 August 1918. However, Vladimir Lenin wanted to spread his policies across Western Europe by marching the Red Army across Poland, to contact the German

Communists. The Supreme Council determined Poland's eastern border in December 1919, but Lenin was worried that the Poles would ally with the White Russians so he offered a new border further to the east to stop them.

Lenin was privately hoping that the over-extension of Poland would lead to its economic collapse and the spread of communism across Europe and even the world. His goal appeared to be coming true when the Western Allies withdrew aid after a right-wing government took over Poland in June 1920. Then a month later, General Mikhail Tukhachevsky announced, 'To the West lies the road to a world-wide wild fire. March upon Vilnius, Minsk, Warsaw and onward to Berlin over the corpse of Poland!'

A new government under Wincenty Witos united Poland as General Haller's troops were driven back across the Vistula River. But then Piłsudski's counter-attack stopped the overstretched Red Army at the gates of Warsaw. Lenin's dream had been dashed and the victory became known as the 'Miracle on the Vistula'.

Fighting continued until an armistice was signed on 12 October 1920, followed by the Treaty of Riga on 18 March 1921. The Polish National Democrat members agreed to let the Soviet Union have the eastern half of Belarus and the Ukraine, a decision which Piłsudski called an act of cowardice. But Poland's extended territories included another five million ethnic minorities and two million Jews. It also left 150,000 ethnic Russians in Poland and one million ethnic Poles in the Soviet Union.

Establishing the Nation

Peace had eventually come to Eastern Europe, but Poland's neighbours were left feeling cheated. The Germans had lost the Polish Corridor, industrial Silesia and the port of Danzig, while the Lithuanians had lost their capital, Vilna. Meanwhile, the Soviets had given up the area known as the Kresy and they were itching to attack again across the border they called the 'Burning Limit'.

After arguing and fighting with its neighbours, Poland could finally settle down, and Józef Piłsudski would be a key figure in the future of the Second Polish Republic. However, he rejected the post of president, believing the constitution to be restrictive, and accepted the role of Chief of the General Staff instead. Gabriel Narutowicz was elected President of Poland in December 1922, only to be assassinated two days later by a man who was hoping to kill Piłsudski. Stanisław Wojciechowski was elected the new president while Wincenty Witos became prime minister, but Piłsudski refused to work with either and retired. The Sanation movement tried to change the focus of politics in his absence by putting national interests ahead of democracy and it resulted in Poland becoming an autocratic state.

Both Berlin and Moscow hoped Poland would fail, and the fall of fourteen governments between November 1918 and May 1926 illustrated how difficult it was to establish a new nation. Both the economy and the currency were weak, while there were regular demonstrations about the high unemployment. Around one in three Poles worked in industry and the majority lived in the western areas. Families in the central and eastern area of the country worked the land. Many farms in the west had been confiscated from their German owners but the properties in the east were owned by Poles who often employed Byelorussians and Ukrainians to work the land.

Piłsudski returned to politics in 1925 but he was dissatisfied with the coalition government and he staged a bloody coup on 12 May 1926. Wojciechowski resigned and Piłsudski refused to accept the presidency for a second time. So Ignacy Mościcki was elected and he appointed Piłsudski his Minister of Military Affairs. He would work to reduce the powers of the parliament and even had eighteen members of parliament arrested when they tried to sack him in 1930.

Difficult Neighbours

Poland rightly believed the Soviet Union wanted to seize its territories, and an alliance with Finland, Estonia and Latvia in March 1922 went some way to ease concerns. Josef Stalin became the General Secretary of the Central Committee in 1924 and he agreed the Treaty of Berlin two years later, under which Germany promised to remain neutral if the Soviet Union invaded Poland.

Germany was accepted into the League of Nations and then blocked Poland's application. Warsaw retaliated by vetoing Berlin's suggestions at the Geneva Economic Convention. The resultant economic war added to Poland's woes, because it relied heavily on German imports. Warsaw then fell out with Czechoslovakia over their mutual border and it refused to join the Little Entente of Czechoslovakia, Romania, and Yugoslavia.

That left France as Poland's only potential ally and foreign ministers Count Eustachy Sapieha and Aristide Briand suggested they should form a defensive alliance against Germany in August 1923. The agreement was reinforced as part of the Locarno Treaties signed in October 1925.

There were anxious times when Piłsudski seized control in May 1926 but the Soviet Union was too busy to take advantage of the situation because of the power struggle between Stalin and Trotsky. Moscow even failed to react when Pytor Voykov, the Soviet foreign minister, was assassinated in Warsaw, for taking part in the execution of Emperor Alexander II and his family in 1918.

France was becoming concerned about the alliance with Poland as tensions were easing with Germany. It demilitarised the Rhineland and then signed a treaty against German aggression as insurance. The Briand-Kellogg Pact of August 1928 eased tensions because France, Germany and Poland promised not go to war to settle any disputes. But the fallout from the Wall Street Crash in 1929 ruined economies and changed the political landscape across Europe. Germany's weak economy suffered more than most and the mainstream parties had no answer for the nation's rising unemployment. The German people turned to the left and right wing for answers and the Nazis started demanding the return of the nation's eastern territories, in particular the Polish Corridor.

President Woodrow Wilson's 'Fourteen Points' had stated that Poland had to have 'free and secure access to the [Baltic] sea'. The Treaty of Versailles had assigned the area west of Danzig to the new nation and the border came into effect in January 1920. The Polish Corridor removed Poland's reliance on trade with Germany but it also cut Germany off from East Prussia, creating arguments for years to come.

Versailles had also declared that the seaport of Danzig was a free city, but the German dock workers refused to unload ammunition for the Polish army during the war with the Soviets. The Polish retaliated by stopping German traffic through the Corridor and so ferries and sealed trains had to be used to connect West and East Prussia. Warsaw also wanted its own port, and it turned the fishing town of Gdynia into a seaport capable of handling half of Poland's imports and exports. Germany wanted the corridor but Poland was adamant they would keep their access to the sea, and in 1931 Warsaw announced it would go to war over the strip of land.

Moscow had been asking for a non-aggression pact in March 1930, but a wary Warsaw took its time to agree. The Treaty of Berlin between Germany and the Soviet Union had been renewed by the time it was signed in July 1932. Tensions between Warsaw and Moscow might have eased but the new pact and the fighting talk over the Polish Corridor upset Berlin.

The Third Reich expanded during 1938 and 1939, until it surrounded Poland on three sides.

Chapter 2

Between Hitler and Stalin

Political unrest, 1933 to 1939

Dealing with Hitler and Stalin

The sequence of political events across Europe between 1933 and 1939 is complicated. The timeline below lists the main events from the Nazis seizing power until the invasion of Poland.

30 January 1933	Adolf Hitler is appointed Chancellor of Germany.
3 February 1933	Hitler states that the Nazis' prime goal is to secure living space or *Lebensraum*.
27 February 1933	The Reichstag building is subjected to an arson attack and the Communist Party is blamed and banned, giving the Nazis a majority.
5 March 1933	The Nazis get 44 per cent of the vote in a new election.
23 March 1933	The Enabling Act allows the Nazis to make laws without consulting the Reichstag for the next four years.
October 1933	Germany withdraws from the League of Nations.
March 1935	Hitler announces that the German Army is to expand and that conscription is going to be introduced.
15 September 1935	The Nuremburg Laws define German citizenship and ban relationships between Aryans and Jews.
7 March 1936	German troops reoccupy the Rhineland.
14 March 1938	The *Anschluss* or Union with Austria. German troops cross the border and Nazi policies are immediately put in place.
30 September 1938	The Munich Agreement agrees that Germany can have the Sudetenland region of Czechoslovakia.

9 November 1938	Jewish shops and synagogues are attacked during *Kristallnacht*, the Night of Broken Glass.
15 March 1939	German troops occupy the rest of Czechoslovakia in contravention of the Munich Agreement.
31 March 1939	Britain guarantees Poland's independence and states it would come to the aid of Poland if Germany invaded.
23 August 1939	The Ribbentrop-Molotov Pact secretly agrees to divide Poland between Germany and the Soviet Union.
25 August 1939	The Anglo-Polish Common Defence Pact, a mutual military assistance agreement, is signed.
1 September 1939	Germany invades Poland from the west.
3 September 1939	Britain and France declare war on Germany.
17 September 1939	The Soviet Union invades Poland from the east.

The Crucial Year 1933

Hitler's appointment as Chancellor of Germany on 30 January 1933 heralded the start of a new era in European politics. A referendum on 5 March increased the Nazis' hold over Germany while the introduction of the Enabling Act on 23 March gave them complete control. The nation then embarked on a course of rearming, reducing unemployment and considering which territories to annex to unite the German people.

Germany was allowed to increase the size of its army and it agreed to join the Four-Power Pact, a peace pact with Italy, France and Britain in return. However, Hitler soon changed his mind and withdrew from the pact and from the League of Nations.

The People Who Led Poland

Ignacy Mościcki was elected president when Józef Piłsudski refused to take the post, following a coup in May 1926. He helped General Edward Rydz-Śmigły oppose Prime Minister Walery Sławek but he was also faithful to Piłsudski until he died in 1935. Mościcki remained as president and he often opposed Rydz-Śmigły's nationalist excesses over the next four years. He escaped to Romania and resigned after Poland was attacked in September 1939. Mościcki was allowed to move to Switzerland in December 1939 and he died there in 1946. He is still the longest serving president in Poland's history.

Piłsudski was only Minister for Military Affairs but he brought national stability to Poland and improved life for the ethnic minorities by opposing the National Democrats' anti–Semitic policies. He agreed a ten–year non–aggression pact with the Soviet Union in January 1934 and then extended the non–aggression pact with Stalin. Hitler then wanted a German-Polish alliance to defy Stalin but Piłsudski turned him down because he wanted to maintain a balance with Poland's neighbours. A revised Polish constitution in April 1935 promised to strengthen the presidency but Piłsudski died before it was implemented.

Józef Beck had been appointed Poland's Minister of Foreign Affairs in 1932 and he had to deal with the nation's changing fortunes over the next seven years. He had negotiated non–aggression pacts with the Soviet Union and Germany by 1934 but Poland's situation deteriorated after Piłsudski died in 1935. Beck wanted to lead an eastern alliance but neither Hungary, Romania, Italy or Yugoslavia wanted to join. He then supported Germany's claim to the Sudetenland in 1938 and engineered the seizure of the Teschen area of Czechoslovakia.

The move alienated Poland from many and it had few friends when Hitler demanded Danzig and the Polish Corridor at the beginning of 1939. So Beck was surprised when Britain and France announced they would defend Poland from an attack by Germany in March 1939. Unfortunately it made Beck overconfident during future diplomatic exchanges with Berlin: he had underestimated Hitler and the strength of the German armed forces. Beck also escaped to Romania when the Wehrmacht invaded Poland in September 1939; he remained under house arrest until he died in June 1944.

Relations with Germany, 1934

Hitler had stated that the Polish Corridor was a 'hideous injustice' during one of his early speeches at the beginning of 1933. Yet only four months later he told Ambassador Alfred Wysocki that Germany had no intentions of seizing the area. Relations between the two countries improved and their customs war ended in September, helping Poland's economy to improve. But there were concerns when Germany withdrew from a disarmament conference and left the League of Nations. They increased when Hitler ordered the building of the Siegfried Line opposite the French border, because it indicated a defensive stance against France.

Both Germany and Poland still thought that the Soviet Union was a threat, so Foreign Minister Konstantin von Neurath and Ambassador Józef

Lipski signed a ten-year non-aggression pact on 26 January 1934. Only four months later, Moscow invited Józef Beck to renew the Polish-Soviet pact.

Relations with France, 1934 to 1936

Each country had differing views because of the threats it faced from their respective neighbours. France saw Germany as the biggest menace and it was hoping to strike a deal with Poland, but it had little to offer because it was still suffering from the world economic crisis. Meanwhile Poland was worried about the Soviet Union, so it was secretly speaking with Germany. Germany wanted a strong Poland, as a buffer zone against the Soviet Union, and it made sense to offer it support. So France was dismayed to hear that Germany and Poland had signed a non-aggression pact in January 1934.

Paris countered by signing a treaty of mutual assistance with Moscow in May 1935. Hitler used this as an excuse to send troops into the Rhineland on 7 March 1936. This show of military strength broke both the Versailles Treaty and the Locarno Treaty, while Hitler was encouraged by the lack of action by France and the League of Nations.

Józef Beck promised Poland would support France but was unable to do much because it was in political turmoil. All Paris could do was to offer Poland a financial loan, so it could increase the size of its armed forces. However, a stock market crash ruined the French economy before most of the money had been handed over and France had to watch as Poland became closer to Germany. Hitler was dismissive of the Polish offer and called the Poles 'the small fish that seek their meat in the wake of a shark'. In other words, he thought they were playing a dangerous game.

Appeasement in the West and Massacres in the East, 1937

Both Britain and France were unprepared for war while their democratic political systems made it unwise to increase their military budgets. Warmongering or overspending would result in a vote of no confidence in the government and an election. Neither country wanted to go to war over Austrian independence or Czechoslovakian territory, so they tried to appease Germany instead. Some even thought that Hitler's early demands to reunite the German people were reasonable.

At the same time, the Nazi dictatorship was able to pursue its economic and military aims without fear of a political backlash from the German people. It was increasing its armed forces and falsifying its budget to hide the true scale of rearmament in Germany. It was also training the people for war through organisations like the Reich Labour Service and the Hitler Youth.

At the same time, the Polish Communist Party was flourishing because many blamed the nation's economic problems on capitalism and democracy. However, Stalin did not trust the Polish communists and over thirty members of the Central Committee were arrested during a visit to Moscow in 1937. They were accused of working for the Polish regime and were either executed or imprisoned. The Polish Communist Party was then disbanded.

Around the same time, the Soviet Union's secret police, the NKVD, started rounding up all ethnic Poles as part of the Great Purge. Nikolai Yezhov branded them potential fifth columnists who had to be removed from the Byelorussian and Ukrainian Socialist Soviet Republics, to make them safe. Ethnic Poles, those suspected of being Polish, and any accused of having Polish sympathies, were targeted. The NKVD even searched telephone books for families with Polish-sounding names. Over 110,000 people would be executed over the next twelve months. Another 140,000 were arrested; the men were worked to death, the women were deported across the Soviet Union and the children were put in orphanages.

Problems over Minorities

The Soviet regime made sure the massacre of the minorities stayed secret. However, the problems that Germany and Poland were having with their ethnic minorities were very public, stirring up resentment on both sides of their border.

The Nazis had established the Population Policy and Racial Welfare Office in 1933 to organise propaganda concerning racial issues. It was renamed the Racial Policy Office in 1935 and it called for 'a long-term change in attitude' over ethnic issues rather immediate action. Dr Walther Gross's staff trained hundreds of ethnic educators and they took exhibitions illustrating the Aryan vision across Germany.

The borders which had been awarded to Poland under the Treaty of Versailles meant that one third of the people belonged to an ethnic minority. Or rather the population of 32 million included over 5 million Ukrainians, 1.5 million Belarusians and 800,000 Germans. Poland had signed the Minorities Treaty in June 1919, so it could join the League of Nations. It had also signed the Riga Treaty with the Soviet Union in 1921, guaranteeing the rights of Ukrainians living in Poland. The Polish constitutions of 1921 and 1935 maintained the spirit of the two treaties, supporting citizen and employment rights, and the freedom to practice their religious, political and cultural activities. They could also run their own churches, social institutions and schools.

Germany had not had to sign the Minorities Treaty because it was an original member of the League of Nations. It meant that the ethnic Poles living in Germany did not have the same rights as ethnic Germans and the loophole was often exploited. Germany and Poland eventually signed a bilateral minorities' agreement in 1934 but neither country supported its conditions.

Many ethnic Germans in the west of Poland backed the Nazis when they came to power, hoping to get their support, but their actions increased anti-German sentiment amongst the Poles. Meanwhile the Ukrainians in the east suffered when Poland's economy faltered, and they sometimes attacked their Polish neighbours in frustration. The country's three million Jews also suffered from a rise in anti-Semitism for the same reason.

The Nazis exploited the fact that established countries, like Germany, had not had to sign up to the Minority Treaties when they discussed their Home to the Reich plan (*Heim ins Reich*). Their intention was to unite ethnic Germans from around the world into a Greater Germany by occupying or invading their neighbours. SS-Obergruppenführer Werner Lorenz opened the Welfare Office for Ethnic Germans in 1937 to establish communication with ethnic Germans living outside the Reich. It sent out correspondence, encouraging them to return home, but also had the power to decide who was an ethnic German, either in the Reich or in occupied areas. The staff could assess the ethnicity individuals, with a view to deporting those who were not.

The Anschluss with Austria, 1938

The Austrian chancellor Kurt von Schuschnigg, and the German ambassador Franz von Papen, signed an agreement on 11 July 1936 to ease tension between their two countries. Hitler met Foreign Minister Konstantin von Neurath, War Minister Field Marshal Werner von Blomberg, Army Commander General Werner von Fritsch, Navy Commander Admiral Erich Raeder and Air Force Commander Herman Göring on 5 November 1937. He told them that Germany was losing the arms race with Britain and France and the only way to reverse the trend was to seize Austrian or Czechoslovakian industries.

Hitler also said they would not find extra living space in either country, so they would have to invade Poland soon afterwards. Blomberg and Fritsch objected, so they were dismissed on 4 February 1938 and Hitler appointed himself Supreme Commander of the Armed Forces in their place. Neurath also objected and he was replaced by Joachim von Ribbentrop.

Hitler presented Schuschnigg with a new set of demands at his Berchtesgaden mountaintop retreat on 12 February. He promised to renew the July 1936 treaty if Nazi sympathisers were appointed to the Austrian government, while Arthur Seyss-Inquart had to be the head of the country's Public Security Ministry. Schuschnigg agreed under duress, but a few days later Hitler announced 'the German Reich is no longer willing to tolerate the suppression of ten million Germans across its borders.'

Schuschnigg asked Britain and France for support but the protests from London and Paris were ignored by Berlin. Violence increased across Austria, so Schuschnigg planned a referendum for 13 March to settle the matter, only he changed the voting rules to swing the result in his favour. So Hitler put the Wehrmacht on standby while Seyss-Inquart replaced Schuschnigg. A forged telegram then asked for German military help to quell the rioting, and troops crossed the border the following morning. They were greeted by many people who welcomed the Union of Germany and Austria.

The Sudetenland

The Anschluss with Austria inspired the German Home Front to take control of the Sudetenland. On 27 March, British Prime Minister Neville Chamberlain stated he would continue to work for peace, but he wanted the Czechs to make concessions. The following day Konrad Henlein met Hitler in secret to discuss how to create the right conditions for the German occupation of the Sudetenland. Henlein's call for Sudeten autonomy at a party congress in Karlsbad on 24 April started the chain of events which would lead to a European political crisis in the autumn.

Hitler told his generals to prepare to invade Czechoslovakia in June 1938, assuring them that neither France nor Britain would take military action. He then demanded control of the Sudetenland because many ethnic Germans lived there. Czechoslovakia was persuaded to cede the area during the Munich crisis of 29 and 30 September. Chamberlain then returned to London and announced that they had made an agreement which guaranteed 'peace for our time'.

Poland had also expressed an interest in the Bohumín area in the east of the country, where many ethnic Poles lived. But Moscow told Warsaw it would end their non-aggression pact if the Poles attacked Czechoslovakia, and the Red Army deployed troops along the Polish border to back up their threat.

Foreign Minister Józef Beck believed Poland should act and an ultimatum was issued to the Czechoslovak government on 30 September. President Edvard Beneš gave in and allowed Polish troops to occupy an 800 km² area where over 225,000 ethnic Poles lived. Beneš was forced to resign a few days later in favour of Hitler's choice: Emil Hácha. Although Poland had gained an area that it thought was theirs, many thought the seizure made Poland an accomplice with Nazi Germany. It had also strained relations with the Soviet Union.

The Polish Corridor

Germany wanted the Free City of Danzig because the majority of the people there were ethnic Germans. There was plenty of nationalist sentiment in Danzig's media but the city's administrator, Albert Forster, said that Poland's frontiers would be respected if the Poles were reasonable. Berlin did, however, want a motorway and a railway connecting Danzig to West Prussia and East Prussia.

Ribbentrop invited Ambassador Lipski to Berchtesgaden on 24 October 1938 to make an agreement over Danzig. He wanted access to the city before Germany would discuss any changes along the Polish-Hungarian border. At the same time, Poland turned down Germany's invitation to join an Anti-Comintern Pact. It also turned down Hitler's offer to extend the 1934 non-aggression pact and even refused extra territory as compensation. The Poles refused because they were concerned that his long-term plan was to send troops into Poland, just like he had done to Austria and Czechoslovakia. The refusals resulted in Hitler telling the German armed forces to prepare to seize Danzig by force. Meanwhile Nazi agitators went to work stirring up ethnic tensions, and violence increased across the city.

The Decision to Attack Poland

The Wehrmacht occupied Bohemia and established a protectorate over Slovakia on 15 March 1939, proving Germany had no desire to stick to the Munich agreement. Hitler was determined to keep expanding the

Third Reich, and both London and Paris believed that it would take force to stop it seizing more territory. The Soviet Union was too far away to make a difference, but Poland would be a useful ally. Romania was also asking Warsaw for help in deterring the Germans but Beck refused to get involved.

Berlin and Warsaw continued to argue over the Polish Corridor in secret, while Hitler ordered the Wehrmacht to concentrate along the Polish border. Poland was looking for allies and Great Britain and France guaranteed to support it on 31 March. Beck immediately went to London to ask for a mutual alliance, but he wanted it to be kept secret so as not to aggravate Hitler. But London announced the Polish-British Common Defence Pact on 6 April, hoping to make Hitler back down; it did not. Germany may have faced the combined forces of Great Britain, France and Poland but the Western Allies were now in a difficult position.

London and Paris wanted to maintain their principles but were desperate to avoid getting involved in a war. Despite the assurances, Poland was unaware that the two countries were unprepared for war and it left Warsaw feeling it was in a position of strength when it dealt with Germany and the Soviets. Poland had also asked for a military loan of £60 million, but Britain had only handed over fifteen per cent of that by August; it would be too little and too late.

Hitler was sure that neither Great Britain nor France would fight for Poland, but he also believed the Poles would not capitulate like Austria or Czechoslovakia had done, so it was time to increase the pressure. The German ambassador for Poland, Hans-Adolf von Moltke, was told to withdraw all proposals to Warsaw and refuse to get into any more diplomatic discussions. Hitler told his military leaders to prepare for war, with a view to invading Poland (codename Case White) soon. He also cancelled the naval treaty with Britain and the non-aggression pact with Poland. Foreign Minister Beck responded defiantly by saying that Warsaw would not give in to Berlin's demands. Hitler was now set on invading Poland.

On 23 May Hitler reminded his military leaders that Germany still needed living space and resources and Poland had them both. His plan was to stir up trouble by getting the media to publish negative stories about oppression of the ethnic Germans living in Poland. He also encouraged discrimination and attacks against the many Polish communities in Germany's eastern areas. Hitler was particularly interested in stirring up trouble in Danzig, and Albert Forster obliged when he took over as the city's Gauleiter in July. The stakes were raised even higher when Germany announced that it was cutting diplomatic links with Poland.

Poland and the Soviet Union

It is now time to see what the Soviet Union thought of Poland. Józef Beck had been worried that Moscow might start meddling in Polish matters when the Soviet Union joined the League of Nations in September 1934, especially after Foreign Minister Vyacheslav Molotov criticised its attitude towards its minorities. But he was being hypocritical because Moscow was planning to have the NKVD arrest, murder and deport its Polish minority.

The Kremlin was sure that Poland supported Germany and it predicted Hitler was planning to seize Austria before dividing Czechoslovakia. It was right. Relations soured during the Czech crisis of September 1938, because Poland demanded the Teschen area and Moscow threatened to attack if Poland seized the area by force. A military crisis was avoided because Czechoslovakia gave into Warsaw's demands.

Warsaw had to turn to Moscow for support when Germany demanded the Polish Corridor a month later. All their treaties were confirmed in return for $20 million of goods, an amount Poland could not afford. The next crisis came when Germany invaded the rest of Czechoslovakia in March 1939, creating the Protectorate of Bohemia and Moravia and an independent Slovak Republic. It left Poland with a pro-Nazi state on its southern border. London and Paris responded by asking Moscow for help in stopping Germany's expansion, leaving a confident Stalin able to dominate the diplomatic discussions.

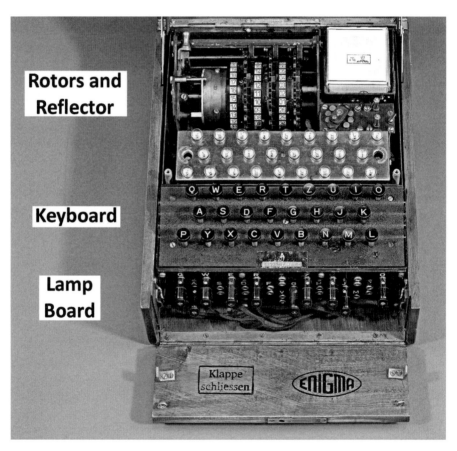

The basic workings of the Enigma coding machine.

Chapter 3

Breaking the German Codes

The Polish Code-breakers and Engima

Enigma and the Cipher Bureau

The Polish military opened a Cipher Section in May 1919 and its cryptologists immediately went to work, deciphering. The Soviets had not changed their codes since the First World War, so it was possible to work out their plans during the War for Independence and defeat the attack on Warsaw in August 1920.

The Warsaw Customs Office received a suspicious package from Germany in the winter of 1927-28 and they found a commercial model of a cipher machine called the Enigma inside. The staff carefully examined the machine and then returned it to the owner, without them knowing.

The Enigma machine had a twenty-six-letter keyboard and twenty-six corresponding lamps which lit up each time a key was pressed. Drums scrambled the typed message by exchanging pairs of letters which had been connected through a plug board. The movement of the rotors meant that the coding changed each time a key was pressed.

A key stroke was passed through the three rotors before it was reflected by a fourth. The reflector would not allow a letter to be reflected on itself before it was passed through the rotors for a second time. The reflector meant that the machine could also decipher coded messages, providing the receiver was using the same set-up. It was also possible to switch keys around with the use of a '*stecker*'. Wires could be connected between keys, so the letters were changed around.

A few months later, the German military started using Enigma but the Cipher Section staff could not read their messages because the military version was an upgraded model. It used six connector leads on the plug board, meaning that the code-breakers had millions of combinations to check.

The Cipher Section merged with the General Staff's cryptography office and the radio intelligence office in 1931, forming the Cipher Bureau under Major Gwido Langer. The head of the German section, Captain

Maksymilian Ciężki, hired three German-speaking mathematics students in September 1932. Marian Rejewski, Jerzy Różycki and Henryk Zygalski had done well on an earlier cryptology course, and they were set the task of deciphering the Enigma messages.

Rejewski had seen a commercial Enigma and he correctly guessed that the QWERTZU keyboard had been replaced by an ABCDEF keyboard. At the same time, French military intelligence handed over the German Enigma settings for September and October 1932, reducing the number of possible combinations dramatically. It allowed Różycki to work out how each rotor revolved at each key press, so replica machines could be built. Meanwhile, Rejewski used pure mathematics to decipher the messages rather than traditional code-breaking techniques. Between them, the three code-breakers were deciphering German military messages by the end of the year.

The Germans started changing the Enigma rotors on a monthly basis, starting in February 1936, and then increased it to a daily basis in October 1936. The number of leads was also increased, making it far more difficult to break the codes. The Cipher Bureau's German section moved to new offices, hidden in the woods in Warsaw's southern suburbs, in 1937, and the challenges kept coming.

Operators were eventually allowed to set the starting positions of the rotors but they had to start a message with a three-letter setting. However, it had to be sent twice (to confirm it), so the receiver set theirs the same. This repeated key combination made it easier to read a message. The sender then turned the rotors to the setting to encrypt the message. The receiver had to reverse the process once to recover the setting and they could then recover the message. The repetition prevented mistakes but it did make it easier to work out the relations between pairs of letters. Operators sometimes typed in common letter combinations which the code-breakers referred to as 'cillies'; in other words, a silly mistake.

The three code-breakers kept improving their deciphering methods, each tackling a different problem, and they were soon able to read most of the messages. Różycki's 'clock' method determined the first rotor, on the right-hand side of the machine. Meanwhile Zygalski designed a system which used twenty-six perforated sheets to replace a card catalogue to speed up the deciphering process. He wrote down the alphabet in twenty-six combinations to represent the first rotor. A square was then split into a 51 by 51 grid and all four sides were lettered from A to Z and then from A to Y to represent the second and third rotors. Holes were made at constant points and sheets were then stacked on top of each other. They were moved around in a set sequence until a possible solution was found. A machine could then be set to decipher other messages.

The fact that six leads connecting six pairs of letters left fourteen letters of the alphabet unchanged was exploited by the team with the use of a device called the 'grill'. However, the Germans changed their procedure again in October 1936, allowing operators to use between five and eight leads, making it far harder to crack the ciphers.

Rejewski built a 'cyclometer' with two sets of Enigma rotors which could create the permutations. That enabled him to write up a card catalogue which was independent of the number of plug connections. It took over a year to write up the thousands of entries but once complete, the operators could quickly identify the rotor settings and daily key. Unfortunately the Germans replaced the Enigma reflector in November 1937, changing all the combinations, but the team had updated the catalogue by the New Year. The Cipher Bureau knew how to break the Enigma, they just needed more staff to keep up with the volume of messages.

The Germans upped the game with the introduction of a new 'indicator procedure' in September 1938, so Rejewski designed a machine to work out settings. The AVA Company built the 'bomba', which could mechanically check hundreds of combinations a minute.

A combination of six bombas and six sets of Zygalski sheets meant the Cipher Bureau could crack the daily keys in just two hours, so they could keep up with the constant flow of messages. Then over the winter of 1938-9 the Germans again changed their system. Two extra leads and two extra rotors were introduced, increasing the number of combinations to an impossible amount. The Cipher Bureau could not afford to build ten times the number of bombas and it would take months to write out the extra sets of Zygalski sheets.

The political situation in Europe intensified over the summer of 1939, as Nazi Germany increased its demands on Poland. On 25 July, Colonel Stefan Mayer, the chief of counter-intelligence of the General Staff's Section II, held an important meeting at the Cipher Bureau's offices. Langer, Ciężki and the three cryptologists explained to British and French code-breakers what they knew about Enigma so far.

France was represented by their radio-intelligence and cryptology chief Major Gustave Bertrand, and Captain Henri Braquenié of the Air Force staff. Britain was represented by the head of the Code and Cipher School, Commander Alastair Denniston, his chief cryptanalyst Dilly Knox, and the head of the Royal Navy's intercept and direction-finding stations, Commander Humphrey Sandwith.

They were all impressed by the headway the Poles had made with Enigma, and they were even more impressed when Mayer offered them the tools to crack the German codes. They were each given a copy of the Enigma machine, one of Rejewski's bombas and a copy of Zygalski's sheets.

Five weeks later, Nazi Germany attacked Poland and it came as no surprise to the Cipher Bureau's staff. They had been listening into the German military's deployment plans in the days leading up to the invasion. But the speed with which the Wehrmacht advanced towards Warsaw did come as a surprise, and instructions to destroy all the equipment and documents were received on 5 September.

Most of the staff headed towards Romania; their truck was seized at the border on 17 September. The three code-breakers managed to reach Bucharest, only to be turned away by the British embassy. They used Gustave Bertrand's codename, Bolek, at the French embassy and transport was arranged to take them to Paris. Those left behind at the Warsaw offices would be arrested and interrogated by the Gestapo but they did not give away the Cipher Bureau's secrets.

Rejewski, Różycki and Zygalski joined a decoding unit at Château de Vignolles in Gretz-Armainvilliers, east of Paris, on 20 October. They worked alongside French, British and Spanish staff at what was codenamed Command Post Bruno or PC Bruno (Poste de Commandement Bruno).

Lieutenant Colonel Gwido Langer visited London and the Code and Cipher School at Bletchley Park in December but he refused to move his staff there. He wanted them where the Polish armed forces were based and that was on French soil. The British cryptanalyst Alan Turing delivered the promised set of Zygalski sheets to PC Bruno instead and the staff immediately started deciphering back-dated Enigma messages. They would be reading Luftwaffe signals in real time by March 1940.

The Wehrmacht and the Luftwaffe changed how they coded their message keys in the spring, but it only took a couple of weeks to crack the new method. France was attacked on 10 May 1940 and the code-breakers had to fly for Algeria when France surrendered to Nazi Germany six weeks later. The international group of code-breakers would return in October, to resume work at Cadix, near Uzès in the Vichy controlled area of France, in October 1940.

Jerzy Różycki and two colleagues, Jan Graliński and Piotr Smoleński, drowned when their passenger ship sank in bad weather in the Mediterranean Sea in January 1942. Rejewski and Zygalski continued to work until German troops entered Vichy France in November 1942. They had done so in response to the Allied invasion of North Africa, Operation Torch.

The code-breakers made a run for it but Rejewski and Zygalski were arrested in the Pyrenees in January 1943. Langer and Ciężki were captured as they tried to cross the Spanish border in March 1943. Ciężki was made a prisoner of war while Langer was sent to work in a slave labour camp in Germany.

Meanwhile, Rejewski and Zygalski had been released and they travelled to Gibraltar, where a plane took them to England in August 1943. Both men were enlisted in the Polish army but they were not allowed to work at Bletchley Park in case German spies were watching them. The two code-breakers spent the rest of the war decrypting low level ciphers at a Polish signals facility in Boxmoor, Hertfordshire. Zygalski would stay in England after the war but Rejewski returned to Poland where he was questioned by the Ministry of Public Security about his wartime work.

Gordon Welchman later said that his team in Hut 6 at Bletchley Park 'would have never got off the ground if we had not learned from the Poles in the nick of time, the details of the Enigma machine and of the operating procedures that were in use.' The information provided by the Polish code-breakers meant that the British Ultra intelligence system had a flying start. Some believe that the contribution may have shortened the war by two years.

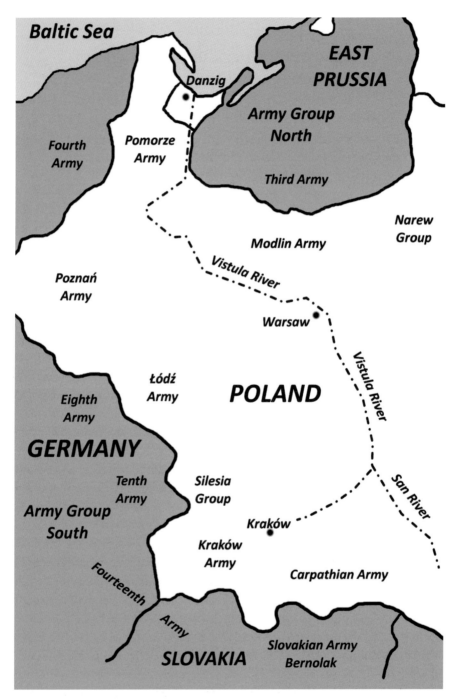

The deployment of Germany's armies against the Polish armies.

Chapter 4

Case White versus Plan West

The Opposing Armies and their Plans

The Wehrmacht's Plan of Attack

Planning had begun on a projected invasion of Poland as early as 1928. Operation Case White (*Fall Weiss*) was developed by Generalfeldmarschall Gerd von Rundstedt, General Major Erich von Manstein and Oberst Günther Blumentritt in the summer of 1939. The attack was organised by the chief of the Army High Command's staff, General Franz Halder, and it was directed by the commander-in-chief of the army, General Walther von Brauchitsch.

The terrain of western and central Poland was suitable for armoured warfare and the plan was to send several spearheads towards Warsaw. Eighth and Tenth Armies would attack from the west, passing north-east through Łódź, while Third and Fourth Armies would advance south, through Mława. They would move fast to cut off and destroy the Polish armies before they could withdraw across the Vistula. Secondary attacks would be made from West Prussia and East Prussia to cut off the troops holding the Polish Corridor. Fourteenth Army and the Slovakian Army Group would make subsidiary attacks through the Carpathian mountain passes, aiming to outflank the troops protecting Kraków.

Nazi Germany's policy of rearmament in the late 1930s meant it had a substantial numeric advantage over the Polish armed forces. Tank detachments would help the infantry break through the border fortifications. Nearly 2,500 tanks, organised into seven panzer divisions and four light divisions, would then lead truck-mounted infantry (*Schützen* or protection regiments) through the breach and spread out behind the Polish lines.

The Luftwaffe deployed around 2,315 aircraft and some of the pilots had combat experience from the Spanish Civil War. The plan was to hit the Polish airfields while the planes were still on the ground, leaving over 750 fighter planes free to patrol the skies. Over 700 bombers would bomb the cities, forcing the civilians to flee into the countryside. Nearly one hundred dive bombers would increase the panic on the roads, interfering with the Polish army's lines of communication.

Army Group Objectives

General Fedor von Bock's Army Group North was split between West Prussia and East Prussia and was supported by the Luftwaffe's First Air Fleet. Frontier troops were deployed along the border between the Lithuanian border and Łomża on the River Narew. General Georg von Küchler's Third Army was to make two attacks from East Prussia. The first would head south past the east side Warsaw, while the second would head west to the Vistula around Chełmno. An eastward advance would link up with General Günther von Kluge's Fourth Army which was moving east from West Prussia. Frontier troops would engage the Polish forces around Gdynia and contain Danzig. The Kriegsmarine's Navy Group East would provide support for the attacks. The small fleet of ships were led by the battleships *Schleswig-Holstein* and *Schlesien*.

Border guards faced the Poznań district because there would be no attack along 200 miles of the border. Rundstedt's Army Group South had the bulk of its force facing the Łódź and Śląsk districts, with the Luftwaffe's Fourth Air Fleet in support. General Johannes Blaskowitz's Eighth Army would advance north-east, passing north of Łódź, approaching Warsaw from the west. General Walter von Reichenau's Tenth Army would advance alongside, passing north of Łódź to approach Warsaw from the south.

General Wilhelm List's Fourteenth Army held a 250-mile-long sector which ran from Upper *Śląsk* following the Slovakian northern border to Hungary. It would advance towards Katowice while the main thrust was made towards Kraków. Part of Fourteenth Army and General Ferdinand Čatloš's Slovakian Army Bernolák would clear the Tatra and Carpathian mountain passes, outflanking Kraków from the east.

The Red Army Order of Battle

The Ribbentrop-Molotov Pact called for the Red Army to cross Poland's eastern border around two weeks after the German invasion in the west. It could then advance to the centre of Poland, meeting the Wehrmacht along the River Bug. However, the Soviet Union had to resolve some border disputes with Japan first. Komandarm Mikhail Kovalyov commanded the Belorussian Front, which covered the 200-mile-wide sector north of the

Pripyat marshes. He had Komkor Vasily Kuznetsov's Third Army, Komdiv Nikifor Medvedev's Eleventh Army and Komkor Ivan Boldin's Cavalry Mechanised Group on his north flank. Komkor Ivan Zakharki's Tenth Army and Komdiv Vasily Chuikov's Fourth Army were on his right flank.

Komandarm Semyon Timoshenko commanded the Ukrainian Front, which covered the 150-mile-wide sector south of the Pripyat marshes. He had Komdiv Ivan Sovetnikov's Fifth Army, Komkor Filipp Golikov's Sixth Army and Komandarm Ivan Tulenev's Twelfth Army under his command. The two armies had a combined strength of 800,000 men.

The Armed Forces of the Republic of Poland

The Polish high command had always considered the Soviet Union to be their biggest threat and most of its divisions were deployed along the eastern border, according to Plan East. Poland had spent huge amounts on building fortifications along the border with the Soviet Union in the 1920s. It spent around one third of its budget on the military but there was never enough to go around. It only had 45,000 regular troops and 200,000 militia when the Nazis came to power in 1933.

The increased warmongering of Germany through the 1930s meant that the Polish military had to do several things. First, it increased the number of regular troops to 283,000 with another 700,000 in reserve. It also deployed most of its strength on its western and northern border under Plan West. But Nazi Germany's occupation of Czechoslovakia in March 1939 called for another redeployment of units along the southern border.

The Polish Army and Plan West

Marshal Rydz-Śmigły had organised the thirty infantry divisions, eleven cavalry brigades, two motorized brigades and three mountain brigades into six armies and six corps-sized groups. He also had nine reserve divisions which would form two armies in reserve. What follows is their deployment, starting in the north-east, moving in an anti-clockwise direction along the border with East Prussia, Germany, Czechoslovakia and finally the Soviet Union.

The Narew Group was deployed in north-east Poland, and it had to stop the Germans crossing the Narew and Biebrza rivers near the Lithuanian border. General Czesław Młot-Fijałkowski had the 18th and 33rd Infantry Divisions as well as the Podlaska and Suwalska Cavalry Brigades to carry out the task.

Brigadier General Emil Krukowicz-Przedrzymirski's Modlin Army had to hold the border with East Prussia for as long as possible. The Nowogródzka and Mazowiecka Cavalry Brigades covered the frontier while the 8th and 20th Infantry Divisions held a fortified line either side of Mława. If necessary they would withdraw behind the Narew and Vistula rivers to defend Warsaw and Płock from the north.

The Pomorze Army was deployed in the Polish Corridor and it had to face both East Prussia and West Prussia to defend Toruń and Bydgoszcz. Lieutenant General Władysław Bortnowski had the 9th, 4th, 15th, 16th and 27th Infantry Divisions and the Pomeranian Cavalry Brigade to hold the difficult position. He organised them into General Mikołaj Bołtuć's East Group and Brigadier General Stanisław Grzmot-Skotnicki's Czersk Group.

The Poznań Army was deployed along the north-west border, facing a defensive area called the Oder Quadrilateral. Major General Tadeusz Kutrzeba deployed the Wielkopolska and Podolska Cavalry Brigades close to the border while the 14th, 17th, 25th and 26th Infantry Divisions covered Poznań.

General Juliusz Rómmel had to deploy the Łódź Army close to the western border to stop the Germans reaching the city. It was important that he held them up long enough for the Prusy Army to deploy south-west of Warsaw. Rómmel deployed the Kresowa and Wołyńska Cavalry Brigade along the border while the 2nd Legions, 10th, 28th and 30th Infantry Divisions were deployed in front of Łódź.

General Antoni Szylling had to defend the south-west border with the Kraków Army. The 6th and 7th Infantry Divisions and the Kraków Cavalry Brigade covered his northern flank, while General Jan Jagmin-Sadowski's Silesia Group covered the important industrial area with the 23rd and 55th Infantry Divisions. General Mieczysław Boruta-Spiechowicz's Bielsko Group had to cover the Tatra Mountain passes with the 21st Mountain Division and the 1st Mountain Brigade. It left Szylling with only 11th Infantry Division and the 10th Motorized Cavalry Brigade in reserve.

Major General Kazimierz Fabrycy's Carpathian Army held the mountain passes along the Czechoslovakian border. The 2nd and 3rd Mountain Brigades had to stop the Germans outflanking the Kraków Army from the south. The switch to Plan West had left General Józef Olszyna-Wilczyński's Grodno Group with little more than a few garrison troops to defend the eastern border with the Soviet Union.

There were insufficient resources to mobilise the entire Polish Army at once, so Rydz-Śmigły planned to group the rest of the divisions in two reserve armies. The Lublin Army would defend the River Vistula south of Warsaw, but the rapid German advance meant that General Tadeusz Piskor did not receive the units allocated to him.

The Prusy Army was supposed to assemble south-west of Warsaw under General Stefan Dąb-Biernacki, ready to cooperate with the Łódź and Kraków Armies. Dąb-Biernacki's plan was to lead the 13th, 19th and 29th Infantry Divisions, Wileńska Cavalry Brigade and 1st Tank Battalion under his Northern Group; he also had the 39th and 44th Infantry Divisions in reserve. General Stanisław Skwarczyński's Southern Group controlled the 3rd Legions, and the 12th and 36th Infantry Divisions. Unfortunately the rapid German advance towards Łódź meant the Prusy Army was under attack before it had finished assembling.

The Polish Air Force

A regiment usually had four squadrons, each with around ten planes; sometimes planes were deployed in smaller escadrilles. The Pursuit Brigade had two fighter squadrons: the 1st Squadrons of the 3rd and 4th Air Regiments. Polish fighter pilots had been given plenty of training, but it all had been in obsolete biplanes. They then had to fly out-of-date 280 PZL P.7s and P.11s because Poland had sold its modern P-24 fighter planes to raise money.

The Bomber Brigade had 2nd, 6th, 10th and 15th Squadrons, the 55th Independent Squadron and two liaison platoons. Again, most of the crews had to fly the outdated 210 PZL.23 (Carp) bombers because there were only thirty-seven modern P-37 (Moose) bombers available. Two liaison platoons, an observation squadron and a staff squadron coordinated their activities. Typically, each army had two fighter squadrons, two observation squadrons and two liaison flights.

Rydz-Śmigły also had over 200 planes organised in two reserve brigades around Warsaw. Altogether Poland had nearly 500 planes but many of them were obsolete models, and they faced the 2,800 up-to-date planes of the Luftwaffe. They would shoot down 134 planes during the battle for Poland, a high number considering the odds, but it was too few to make a difference.

The Polish Navy

The Polish Navy was commanded by Counter-Admiral Józef Unrug and organised by Chief of Staff Vice-Admiral Jerzy Świrski. Poland had a short Baltic coast with the harbours of Gdynia and Hel. It had bought four destroyers, five submarines and various support vessels and mine sweepers but they were vastly outnumbered by the German Navy (*Kriegsmarine*). The Navy was organised into the Land Command and the Naval Command in July, and together they comprised the Coastal Defence Group.

With British agreement, three of Poland's destroyers sailed for Britain under Operation Peking just before the Germans attacked. That left the Minelayer *Neck*, the destroyer *Gale* and six minesweepers named after birds. The five submarines were called *Wolf*, *Wildcat*, *Lynx*, *Vulture* and *Eagle*. They were supported by several torpedo boats and auxiliary vessels. Two squadrons of obsolete seaplanes provided air cover for the ships.

Colonel Dąbek's Land Command had 15,000 men to defend naval bases and depots along the coast. The Hel peninsula was protected by 3,000 men, another 200 men were deployed at Westerplatte ammunition depot while the Border Defence Corps defended Hel and Gdynia. The Polish Navy was also responsible for the River Pripyat in the Pinsk marshes. Several monitors were built or bought to support the Border Defence Corps along the River Vistula.

The division of Poland's territories under the Ribbentrop-Molotov secret deal.

Chapter 5

Treacherous Neighbours

The Ribbentrop-Molotov Pact, August 1939

The Danzig Problem

Bohemia was made a German protectorate and Slovakia proclaimed its independence on 14 March 1938, leaving Poland with pro-German territories to its north, west and south. Hitler's next objective was Danzig, but Beck refused to negotiate over it. Ribbentrop said that anti-German demonstrations were harming relations between their two counties on 26 March, but Lipski said Poland would never let Germany have the free city. Ribbentrop dismissed Lipski, and the two foreign ministers would not meet again until the day before Germany attacked.

Poland on the Eve of World War II

Polish leaders were confident about their country's situation in the summer of 1939 and propaganda made sure that the people shared their view. However, the rest of Europe's view was far from positive. The Poles thought their economy was healthy while other countries thought it was weak. They also thought living standards were improving while visitors thought they were backward. Poland might have had a million-strong army with another million in the reserves but its annual military budget was only two per cent of Germany's massive expenditure on arms.

The leaders of the major political parties believed Poland was politically stable but the minor parties refused to take part in elections because of their authoritarian nature. There was also a variety of problems with the minorities, particularly ethnic Germans, while nationalism and anti-Semitism were on the rise.

Poland was also running out of friends by the summer of 1939. Warsaw thought it had a strong ally in France, but Paris was concerned about getting dragged into any arguments with Germany over the Polish Corridor. Britain's pledge of support against an attack by Germany only increased Poland's confidence in late August.

Operation Tannenberg

Security Service agents started recruiting ethnic Germans in Poland into paramilitary Self-Protection units (*Selbstschutz*) in October 1938. Some were trained in sabotage and partisan activities in Germany while the rest were taught about Nazi policies and encouraged to provoke anti-Polish feelings. Members spent the winter forwarding information which might be useful to the German military during an invasion. They also collected the names of the Polish intelligentsia, so the Gestapo's Central Unit IIP (Poland) could list them in the Special Prosecution Book. It was issued to *SS*-Sturmbannführer Rudolf Tröger ready to launch Operation Tannenberg. The Gestapo and Special Service would locate them, the Criminal Police would round them up and firing squads would execute them at remote locations. The Gestapo had also assembled a list of Polish activists living across Germany. Around 2,000 would be arrested and murdered just before the attack on Poland was launched.

The Peking Plan

The head of the British Military mission, Lieutenant General Sir Adrian Carton de Wiart, failed to convince Rydz-Śmigły to deploy the Polish armies further back from the border following the signing of the Polish-British Common Defence Pact. He did, however, convince him to send most of the Polish fleet out of the Baltic Sea before the German Navy blocked the Danish straits.

They agreed three destroyers would sail to Britain, so they could escort ships loaded with supplies to Romanian ports in the Black Sea, fulfilling Britain's promise to support Poland. Counter-Admiral Unrug wrote out the Peking Plan on 26 August and the sealed envelopes containing the orders were delivered to the ships *Thunder*, *Lightning* and *Storm*.

Commander Roman Stankiewicz received the instruction 'Execute Peking' three days later and the three ships set sail for the North Sea, followed by German reconnaissance planes. They changed course as soon as it was dark and were soon intercepted by the Royal Navy destroyers HMS *Wallace* and *Wanderer*. The three destroyers soon docked in Leith, the port of Edinburgh, and they would take part in many engagements during the war. The rest of the Polish Navy's vessels were either sunk or captured in the first few days after the invasion.

The Polish Defence Plan

Both Britain and France had pledged their support for Poland in July, but the Polish politicians and generals were arguing over how to deploy the armies.

The generals wanted to deploy them behind the Vistula and San rivers in central Poland, giving time to assemble the divisions while reconnaissance units monitored the Wehrmacht's progress. Marshal Rydz-Śmigły could then organise counter-attacks against the enemy's weakest points.

However, the politicians wanted to deploy the troops close to the border, to stop the Germans capturing the nation's resources and industries in the first few days. They were concerned that the Wehrmacht would just occupy the border areas before the Nazis demanded a peace treaty, as they had done to Czechoslovakia.

The politicians won the argument, leaving the generals to prepare new defences close to the border and considering how to withdraw to the existing fortifications if the time came. It left the Polish divisions stretched thin along the border, but the people remained undaunted by Hitler's threats because the government assured everyone that the German invasion could be stopped.

The politicians believed their own propaganda because the generals had promised them that their armies could keep the Germans at bay for six months. The British and French were more conservative in their estimates, but they believed Poland could hold the Germans back for at least two months, with the fighting ending in trench warfare. Either estimate would give Poland's western allies time to send reserves.

The Ribbentrop-Molotov Pact

Hitler may have hated the Soviets, but trade between their countries was advantageous to both. Moscow needed German technology and equipment to fulfil its Five-Year Plan while Germany needed Soviet raw materials to build its armed forces. Hitler also ended the non-aggression pact with Poland and the naval agreement with Britain when Britain and France guaranteed Polish independence in March 1939.

Stalin replaced his Foreign Minister Maxim Litvinov with Vyacheslav Molotov in May 1939. He started public negotiations with Britain and France in mid-June but was also ordered to start secret talks with Germany only a month later. Molotov dragged out the discussions with Britain and France because he insisted that Soviet troops had to be allowed to cross the

Polish border if Germany attacked Poland. Józef Beck refused because he thought the Red Army would never leave Polish soil.

The public talks were getting nowhere but the Soviets and Germans came to an economic agreement at the beginning of August. Kliment Voroshilov then suspended talks with Britain and France as the military talks with the Soviets began. Ribbentrop proposed dividing Poland into two on 21 August and the following day Hitler told his military commanders about his plans to exterminate the Poles:

> *The object of the war is to physically destroy the enemy. That is why I have prepared for the moment only in the East, my Death's Head formations with orders to kill without pity or mercy all men, women, and children of Polish descent or language. This is the only way we can obtain the living space we need.*

The same day, London and Paris announced they were prepared to go to war if German troops crossed the Polish border. Hitler thought neither could do anything because they were too far away to help. He had also sent Ribbentrop to Moscow, where he and Molotov signed a non-aggression pact on 23 August.

There was surprise around the world when the news was released, and *Time* magazine called it the 'Communazi Pact'. Soviet propaganda minimised its past differences with Nazi Germany, and while many breathed a sigh of relief at the ten-year agreement, no one knew the pact had a secret clause which divided Poland into two. The plan was for Germany to attack first from the west on 26 August, followed by a Soviet attack from the east a few days later. The clause also assigned Lithuania to Germany and Finland while Estonia and Latvia would go to the Soviets.

Hitler instructed his generals to prepare to invade Poland, telling them, 'Our enemies are small worms. I saw them at Munich.' He also told Sir Nevile Henderson, the British ambassador in Berlin, that Germany no longer faced a war on two fronts and it was time to accept his demands. Prime Minister Chamberlain's government responded on 25 August by promising to defend Poland.

Mobilisation

Great Britain and France urged Poland not to fully mobilise, so as not to aggravate Germany, unaware that the Wehrmacht was already deployed in force along the border. Beck ordered mobilisation to begin in earnest on 29 August, but British and French diplomats still meddled in the process. The interference delayed Polish military plans by another twenty-four hours, so that only thirty out of forty divisions were mobilised by 1 September. Poland may have had a one million strong army but half of it was in the wrong place when the attack started.

The Wehrmacht's Plans

The German invasion was timed to begin at 4 am on 26 August but the signing of the Polish-British Common Defence Pact made Hitler hesitate. The *Wehrmacht*, *Luftwaffe* and *Kriegsmarine* were told to wait until the same time on 1 September, while sabotage units along the border were told to postpone their activities until the night of 31 August. One unit did not get the order and Berlin explained away the attack on the Jablunkov Pass border post as the act of an 'insane individual'. Hitler spent the day trying to convince the British and the French not to get involved in Polish affairs. Despite his outward display of concern, he privately believed that they could not (or would not) do anything, even if they did declare war in support of Poland.

The Polish intelligence unit in Paris, codename *Lecomte*, had been listening into the Ribbentrop-Molotov talks since 22 August. They reported that the Wehrmacht intended to halt along the old border between Prussia and Russia, without realising that it referred to the secret part of the pact which would divide Polish territory between Germany and the Soviet Union. Planes had also been spotted flying reconnaissance missions into Polish airspace, while there were numerous reports of troop movements along the border. They all pointed to one thing: war!

Germany made demands over Danzig and the Polish Corridor late on 29 August, on the pretence of protecting the ethnic Germans living in these areas. Germany wanted immediate control of Danzig but it suggested holding a vote on the future of the Polish Corridor. It would be a rigged referendum, because any Poles who had lived in the area for less than twenty years would not be allowed to vote while Germans who had been born there but were now living elsewhere could. Germany would get access to East Prussia via an autobahn if Poland won. Germany would get the corridor if it won, and the port of Gdynia would become an enclave connected to Poland by an autobahn.

Ribbentrop read the German proposal to Sir Nevile Henderson late on 30 August, but he refused to hand over a copy to forward to Warsaw.

Instead, he insisted on handing it to the Polish representative in person. The Polish Ambassador, Józef Lipski, eventually arrived late on 31 August, only to tell Ribbentrop that he did not have the power to sign an agreement. So Ribbentrop ended the meeting and German radio announced that Poland had refused his offer. The Luftwaffe started bombing Poland a few hours later.

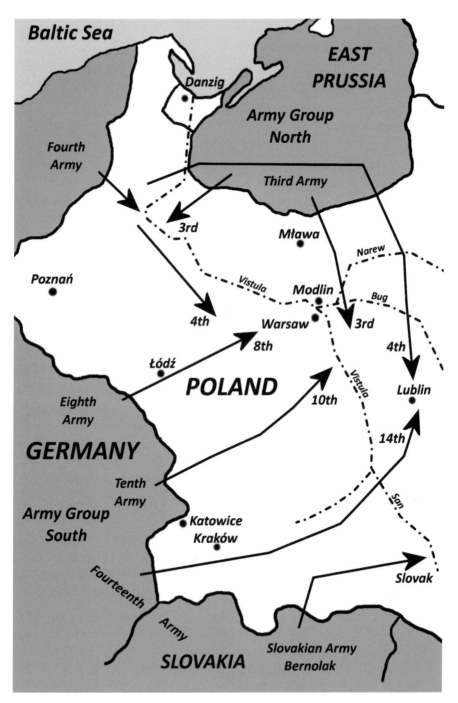

The Wehrmacht's advance across Poland during the first two weeks of September 1939.

Chapter 6

Speak the Same Language

The Invasion of Poland, September 1939

Operation Himmler

Nazi Germany would not make a formal declaration of war, instead it planned covert operations to make it look like the Poles had attacked first. Operation Himmler was devised by the head of the Reich Security Office, Reinhard Heydrich, and the raids were organised by his assistant Heinrich Müller. SS and SD men dressed in Polish uniforms would attack locations along the border and concentration camp prisoners (codenamed Canned Goods), also in Polish uniforms, would be shot and left at the scene.

Apart from the delay of 25/26 August, the rest of Operation Himmler was carried out according to plan late on 31 August 1939. The largest attack was made against Gleiwitz radio station in south-east Germany, where Alfred Naujocks' team broadcast an anti-German message in Polish.

The Luftwaffe started their bombing attacks as soon as it was light, while the ships stationed off the Westerplatte opened fire. Attacks were then made all along the border, from East Prussia, West Prussia, against Silesia and through the Carpathian mountain passes. They came from the north-west, the south-west and the south and they were all heading for Warsaw, in the heart of Poland. Hitler later listed twenty-one Polish attacks across the German border in a statement justifying the invasion. He then said, 'I have resolved to speak to Poland in the same language that Poland has used toward us for several months.' In other words, accusations of minor acts of Polish violence had been countered with a military invasion.

Both Britain and France would declare war on Germany on 3 September but neither could do anything to support Poland because, as Hitler had rightly calculated, they were too far away. All France could do was man its border while Britain prepared supplies to be shipped via the Mediterranean.

The Baltic Battles

The German Navy attacked several targets along the Baltic coast. The Polish military had an ammunition depot on the Westerplatte peninsula, at the mouth of the River Vistula north of Danzig. The battleship *Schleswig-Holstein* opened fire early on 1 September while marines went ashore and engineers attacked from the land side; they were all driven back. The depot was repeatedly shelled, bombed and attacked but Major Henryk Sucharski's 180-strong garrison held out until 7 September.

Sub-Lieutenant Konrad Guderski had trained his fifty-six staff to defend Danzig's post office. They drove off attacks by the police, SS and SA units for most of 1 September. Only four escaped and the rest were executed a month later.

The Luftwaffe began bombing the Hel peninsula on 1 September and around fifty planes were shot down as they targeted the Polish ships off the coast. So the rest of the ships put their crews and guns ashore, ready to fight alongside the infantry. Fourth Army attacked eight days later and Captain Stanislaw Zwartynski's command was the only one still fighting in northern Poland. Admiral Unrug eventually surrendered the 2,800-strong garrison on 1 October because they had run out of supplies.

The Polish defences around Gdynia were overrun during the capture of the Polish Corridor, so Colonel Stanisław Dąbek withdrew the garrison to the Oksywie Heights, on 8 September, to avoid civilian casualties. They fought on until the ammunition ran out four days later and then Dąbek gave the order to cease fire before committing suicide.

Three destroyers had escaped to Britain under Operation Peking but the rest of the Polish Navy did what they could to protect the harbours. The minelayers *Mewa* and *Gryf* went out to sea on 1 September to lay a mine barrier to protect the port of Gdynia. However, Operation Rurka had to be abandoned after the Luftwaffe damaged both ships. The five submarines of the Polish Navy were supposed to stop the Germans landing around Gdynia or on the Hel peninsula but the deteriorating situation on land meant they had to scatter. Two would make the long journey to Britain but the rest were interned by Sweden.

Army Group North

Bock had two initial objectives. Third Army would advance from East Prussia, approaching Warsaw from the east. It would also cut the Polish Corridor in a pincer attack by Fourth Army. Part of Fourth Army would then attack Modlin Fortress, north of the capital, while the rest made a flanking move across East Prussia to cover Third Army's left flank.

Third Army, from East Prussia to Warsaw

Third Army advanced across the East Prussian border to attack the Modlin Army on 1 September. The Wodrig Corps could not outflank the Polish position along the Narew marshes, so it was down to I Corps and Panzer Division Kempf to break through the fortifications around Mława. A bungled counter-attack by 20th Infantry Division and fifth column attacks resulted in General Krukowicz-Przedrzymirski ordering a withdrawal. The Modlin Army and the Narew Group were then attacked by Luftwaffe as they fell back to the Narew and Vistula rivers and rallied alongside the Wyszków Group. The Modlin and Narew Groups then headed for Warsaw while the Wyszków Group withdrew south-east only to be destroyed in the battle of Tomaszów Lubelski.

Meanwhile XXI Corps had advanced west across the base of the Polish Corridor, bypassing the Pomorze Army group defending the River Vistula. General Mikołaj Bołtuć had to abandon Grudziądz and head south-east on 3 September after hearing that Fourth Army had crossed the Vistula at Chełmno.

The Pułtusk bridgehead was holding on north of Warsaw, but the men covering the Różan bridgehead abandoned the World War I forts along the River Narew by mistake. The cutting of the Polish Corridor and the loss of the Mława position meant that the XIX Panzer Corps and the XXI Corps could attack the Narew bridgeheads.

A force of only 500 men stopped the 10th Panzer Division crossing the River Biebrza at Wizna for three days. German planes had dropped leaflets urging the Poles to surrender but Captain Władysław Raginis swore to fight on. The badly injured Raginis committed suicide when his men ran out of ammunition. Their brave actions gave the Narew Group time to withdraw onto the Polesie Group. The XIX Panzer Corps then outflanked the Łomża bridgehead and headed south towards Brześć, allowing XXI Corps to cross the River Narew.

The rest of the Modlin Army continued its fighting withdrawal towards Warsaw and while some men entered the Modlin Fortress on 13 September, the rest headed for the Romanian border. They would be defeated by Red Army troops at the battle of Tomaszów Lubelski, north of Lwów.

Meanwhile Third Army had moved past the east side of Warsaw by 15 September and began attacking the Praga district of the city on the east bank of the Vistula.

Fourth Army, West Prussia to Modlin Fortress and Brześć

General Bortnowski felt the Polish Corridor was vulnerable to attack from two directions, but he still had to defend it with the Pomorze Army. Fourth Army's attack from West Prussia started on 1 September, but late the following evening, ethnic Germans dressed in Polish uniforms spread rumours that the Pomorze Army was in retreat. The people of Bydgoszcz fled as the fifth columnists started firing into crowds. Dozens of ethnic Germans were dragged from their homes and killed in what became known as Bloody Sunday. But they had achieved their objective, because the thousands of refugees blocked the bridges over the Vistula.

Nazi propaganda exaggerated the incidents, stirring up resentment, while hundreds of civilians were taken hostage; around 700 were executed. A secret decree issued on 4 October stated that past war crimes would not to be prosecuted. Soon afterwards, many more were shot in the Valley of Death, north-east of the town, as part of Operation Tannenberg.

Elsewhere, General Guderian had to step in because XIX Panzer Corps was held up by Polish cavalry units. Meanwhile, the rest of XIX Panzer Corps had helped II Corps defeat the Czersk Group around Tuchola by 5 September, prompting Hitler to visit Guderian to congratulate him. The survivors of the Pomorze Army then fell back towards Warsaw and came under the Poznań Army.

Fourth Army now split into two, with part moving fast through East Prussia before turning towards Brześć on Third Army's left flank. Guderian's tanks were approaching the city from the north when the Red Army crossed the border on 17 September, and moved towards the fortress from the east. General Konstanty Plisowski's group withdrew into the Pinsk marshes while General Franciszek Kleeberg's group headed towards Warsaw, only to hear en route that it fallen. The two generals then headed towards Kielce, only to hear the Polish army had surrendered before they reached its main arsenal at Dęblin.

The rest of Fourth Army had attacked the huge Modlin Fortress north of Warsaw on 13 September. It found the rump of the Modlin and Pomorze Armies waiting for them. For two weeks, anti-aircraft batteries shot down the Luftwaffe's planes while General Wiktor Thommée's men defended the perimeter with the help of the armoured train 'Death'. However, news from the rest of the country convinced Thommée that it was time to surrender, but Rochus Misch was shot at and wounded when he tried to contact the Germans. Tensions increased when over 600 soldiers and civilians were massacred during a cease-fire, but 24,000 troops eventually surrendered when the fortress capitulated on 29 September.

Army Group South

There was a 200-mile gap between the two army groups, where the Germans chose not to attack, and it was covered by fortifications, including the Oder Quadrilateral. The Poznań Army had one of the few Polish Army's successes in the area, in what were otherwise dark times for Poland. The Wielkopolska Cavalry Brigade raided Fraustadt on 2 September in a small but morale-boosting attack across the German border.

Rundstedt had two armies ready to advance north-east past Łódź, approaching Warsaw from the south-west. Part of his Third Army would approach Kraków from the west and cross the Carpathian Mountains, supported by a Slovakian army.

Eighth Army, Breslau to Warsaw

Eighth Army crossed the border near Breslau (now Wrocław) and advanced north-east past Łódź, heading straight for Warsaw. General Blaskowitz thought the Poznań Army had already withdrawn to the capital by train, so he had taken few precautions to cover his left flank. General Tadeusz Kutrzeba had, in fact, joined the Pomorze Army and General Bortkowski was leading them back towards the capital.

Eighth Army overran the Piotrków Group as it assembled north-east of Łódź on 8 September, delaying the advance on Warsaw, and so Bortkowski took the opportunity to counter-attack across the Bzura River. His troops struck the German columns in 'the bloodiest and most bitter battle of the entire Polish campaign'.

Fourth and Tenth Armies were reinforcing Eighth Army when the Polish generals heard that the Łódź Army was heading for Modlin Fortress, so they decided to head the same way. The remnants of Poznań Army and the Pomorze Army disengaged Eighth Army, withdrew into the Kampinos Forest and headed for Warsaw or Modlin Fortress.

Tenth Army

The Wołyńska Cavalry Brigade ambushed 4th Panzer Division in the Mokra woods on 1 September, capturing fifty tanks with the help of two armoured trains. The rest of XVI Corps broke through Łódź Army at Częstochowa the following day, so General Juliusz Rómmel ordered a withdrawal towards the capital. Some did not get the order and fought on, against General Erich Hoepner's 600 tanks, until they were overrun. The Łódź Army's withdrawal meant the Prusy Army and the Kielce Group did not have time to mobilise around Radom. Units had to be deployed piecemeal and while some were defeated at Piotrków and Tomaszów Mazowiecki, the rest were overrun at Iłża. Only 70,000 soldiers of the Prusy Army had escaped across the Vistula, south of Warsaw, by 9 September.

The capital had been under air attack since 1 September and the small number of troops, fire fighters and volunteers were soon joined by various units escaping the advancing German columns. Marshal Rydz-Śmigły gave command of the makeshift Warsaw Army to General Rómmel as Tenth Army approached west. General Walerian Czuma set up a Defence Command in in the city and Civilian Commissar Stefan Starzyński organised the Civil Guard, but the civilian services were told to leave the city.

They XVI Panzer Corps lost another eighty tanks fighting through the southern suburbs, and then General Reichenau found his flank was under attack as the Poznań and Pomorze Armies counter-attacked across the River Bzura. The tanks of the 1st and 4th Panzer Divisions counter-attacked on 16 September and air attacks forced them to abandon their heavy equipment. Few Polish units escaped through the Kampinos Forest into Warsaw, but they had stalled the advance on Warsaw, giving the garrison time to organise its defences. Altogether there was a sizeable force of twenty-five infantry battalions and forty tanks around the capital by the time they were surrounded on 13 September. Repeated attacks cut Modlin Fortress off from Warsaw on 22 September. The city capitulated on 28 September and the huge defensive position surrendered the following day.

Tenth Army helped Fourteenth Army attack what remained of the Modlin and Lublin Armies south-east of Warsaw. Generals Emil Krukowicz-Przedrzymirski and Stefan Dąb-Biernacki wanted to escape to either Hungary or Romania but the roads south-east of Lublin were blocked and they had to surrender. The Polesie Group was also tracked down and forced to surrender on 6 October because it had run out of ammunition.

Fourteenth Army

The VIII Corps attacked the Silesia and Bielsko Groups either side of Katowice, outflanking a fortified area, while paramilitary units attacked Polish units holding the Silesian industrial areas. A plan to draw the Germans into a trap resulted in defeats around Woźniki and Oświęcim (later renamed Auschwitz by the Germans) on 2 September. It meant that General Szylling had to order the rest of the Kraków Army to withdraw towards Kraków and the Vistula. The Luftwaffe disrupted the withdrawal and Szylling lost contact with his command while his men had to abandon their heavy equipment.

The Kraków Army split into the Jagmin and Boruta Groups but they were both pushed back astride the River Vistula and Kraków city was abandoned on 6 September. The rapid withdrawal did not give Major General Piskor time to assemble the Lublin Army along the River Vistula south of Warsaw. It was soon driven back, allowing Fourteenth Army to concentrate on crushing the remnants of the Prusy Army. The Lublin Army then fell back to join the Kraków Army in a final battle around Tomaszow Lubelski.

The Carpathian Army faced problems along Poland's south border because there had not been time to build enough fortifications following the occupation of Slovakia. The troops defending the Sola valley in the Tatra Mountains held on despite being heavily outnumbered. The 1st Mountain Brigade was eventually told to withdraw because of breakthroughs elsewhere, but the bunkers around Węgierska Górka never received the order and fought on until they were overrun.

The 10th Motorized Cavalry Brigade knocked out around fifty tanks as XVIII Panzer Corps crossed the Tatra Mountains via the Jabłonka Pass, and advanced over fifty miles in four days, compromising the Kraków Army's flank. General Szylling realised that Fourteenth Army was stretched as his men fell back towards Warsaw, so he attacked around Tomaszów Mazowiecki on 18 September in the biggest tank battle of the invasion. But General List's formations were too strong and while Szylling's men escaped, General Piskor was forced to surrender the remains of Lublin Army when they counter-attacked.

The Carpathian Army joined the Kraków Army (they were renamed the Małopolska Army) as it fell back and they suffered many casualties escaping across the River San. The survivors were either captured or killed during the battle of Lwów which ended on 20 September.

The garrison of Przemyśl Fortress stopped Fourteenth Army's advance across southern Poland until the Germans discovered they could cross the

San north of the city on 11 September. There was panic as the city was evacuated but 10th Motorized Cavalry Brigade contained the bridgehead until General Kazimierz Sosnkowski gave the order to withdraw on 14 September.

Sosnkowski was appointed commander of what remained of the southern armies and they were heading east for Lwów when they heard the Red Army had crossed the border on 17 September. Sosnkowski had to tell his men to head for the Hungarian border but few of them reached it.

Polish units had poured into Lwów as Fourteenth Army approached and they ignored the German propaganda leaflets dropped by the Luftwaffe urging them to surrender. That was until the Red Army crossed the border on 17 September. Rundstedt was ordered to withdraw on 20 September, leaving it down to the Soviet Sixth Army to accept General Franciszek Sikorski's surrender. Sikorski and many of his brother officers would be executed in the Katyń massacre in 1940, while the rest were sent into the Soviet Main Camp Administration; the Gulag.

The Siege of Warsaw

The Luftwaffe started daily bombing raids against Warsaw on 1 September and the biggest raid on the 10th was referred to as 'Bloody Sunday'. The city's anti-aircraft defences shot down many planes but many of the guns were damaged by the Stuka dive bombers. The garrison initially welcomed the arrival of units which were falling back ahead of the Germans but they were often short of ammunition and had lost much of their equipment.

Third Army closed in from the east, Fourth Army from the north-west and Eighth Army from the south-west. The ground attacks began on 8 September and the number of German troops increased as the days passed, until around 250,000 troops and 1,000 artillery pieces had surrounded Warsaw. Day after day the artillery shelled the suburbs and the Luftwaffe flew overhead as infantry and tanks cleared city block after city block. The ground troops regrouped after Modlin Fortress, north of Warsaw, was cut off on 22 September and then General Blaskowitz stopped the attack while his units regrouped.

The ground attacks were renewed after the Luftwaffe dropped over 600 tons of bombs on the city on 25 September, what was called 'Black Monday'. The forts at Mokotów, Dąbrowski and Czerniaków had fallen by the time Generals Rómmel and Czuma agreed a cease fire on 27 September. The number of civilian casualties had been rising rapidly due to lack of food and medical supplies and they feared a humanitarian crisis.

The garrison destroyed all their larger weapons but they hid a lot of their pistols, rifles and grenades and many would be later unearthed by underground units. Over the days that followed, around 140,000 Polish soldiers were escorted to prisoner of war camps while the German security forces moved in. They immediately set to work arresting and executing the members of the intelligentsia on their lists.

The Soviet Invasion

Nazi leaders wanted the Red Army to attack Poland as soon as the Wehrmacht had crossed the Polish border. The German ambassador Friedrich Werner von der Schulenburg was asking Moscow to join in the battle but the Foreign Minister Vyacheslav Molotov took his time because the Soviet Union was engaged in border disputes with Japan. The Red Army also needed the time it took the Germans to defeat Poland to mobilise its troops.

A ceasefire with Japan came into force on 16 September, and Molotov delivered the declaration of war to the Polish Ambassador in Moscow, Wacław Grzybowski, the following day. It said, 'the capital of Poland, Warsaw, no longer exists. The Polish Government has disintegrated and no longer shows any sign of life. This means that the Polish State and its Government have, in point of fact, ceased to exist.'

The Red Army crossed the border on 17 September and while it had broken the Soviet-Polish Non-Aggression Pact, Moscow considered that Poland did not exist as a nation anymore. As far as it was concerned, it was protecting the Belarusians and Ukrainians who lived in Poland's eastern territories. A few Polish cities thought the Red Army were just marching through to attack the Germans. Communists and Jews saw them as their liberators, Belarusians and Ukrainians saw them as their protectors, and the Polish General Rómmel went as far as to say the Soviets were the Poles' ally.

The Border Defence Corps had been building fortifications since 1936 but they were not ready by the time most of the troops were sent to the west in the summer of 1939. Only the 20,000 men of the Border Defence Corps were left by the time the Soviets attacked and the rest of the Polish army had either been overrun, was gathering around Warsaw, or was fighting its way towards the Romanian Bridgehead.

President Ignacy Mościcki and Prime Minister Felicjan Składkowski wanted Marshal Rydz-Śmigły to abandon the eastern borders and to use his troops to fight off the Germans. The Polish government crossed into

Romania the day after the Soviet invasion but many units failed to get the order to follow their leaders over the border. They fought on with differing outcomes; some were rapidly overrun while others fought on for several days.

General Józef Olszyna-Wilczyński and the mayor of Grodno Roman Sawickibegan defended Grodno for several days withthe help of militia, volunteers, scouts and police. The survivors of the attack escaped towards the Lithuanian border but Olszyna-Wilczyński's car was stopped by Soviet troops and he was executed.

Only 9,000 men assembled north of Lublin and General Wilhelm Orlik-Rueckemann led them north, passing between the advancing German and Soviet units. He thought an engagement would raise morale, so he made his men dig in and then encouraged the Soviets to attack. The Poles defeated them on 28 September and then headed south. The Red Army caught them three days later, only this time they were tired and short of ammunition, so the 3,000 survivors escaped into the forests.

General Władysław Anders' cavalry force was also intercepted on 27 September, as it headed for the Romanian Bridgehead. He was wounded while his tired men tried to escape through the forests around Przemyśl. Anders was one of the few high-ranking Polish officers to survive the Katyń massacre.

The Polesie Group had been successfully defending Brest-Litovsk from Guderian's panzers since 14 September. However, the Soviet invasion, three days later, threatened to cut it off, so General Kleeberg first tried to get to the Romanian border and then to Warsaw. He reached neither but collected supplies in Dęblin before moving into the forests near the Świętokrzyskie Mountains. The 18,000-strong force fought the Red Army until it ran out of ammunition on 5 October; it was the last regular Polish unit to surrender.

Guderian's troops took several days to clear Brest-Litovsk and some went further than the agreed demarcation line. The 29 Tank Brigade met them twenty miles north of the city on 20 September and the soldiers toasted each other while the commanders exchanged pleasantries. Guderian was irritated to hear that he had to leave the city and its fortress and then withdraw behind the Bug River. The Soviet and German generals saluted each other's troops as they marched past and Guderian then withdrew his troops. It would take the Wehrmacht several weeks and thousands of casualties to capture the fortress, at the start of Operation Barbarossa in June and July 1941.

The Red Army reached the agreed border along the Narew, Western Bug, Vistula and San rivers on 28 September, the same day that Warsaw capitulated. The remnants of the Polish army were scattered, and the final surrender took place on 6 October. Casualties had been relatively light on both sides, but tens of thousands (numbers vary) of Poles had been captured. The Soviets executed many officers, including General Olszyna-Wilczyński, on the spot, while the rest were separated from their men and taken into captivity for political evaluation.

France and Britain gave a low-key response to the Red Army's attack because it did want to antagonise the Soviet Union. The publicised version of the Polish-British Common Defence Pact, which had been announced on 25 August 1939, had promised to help Poland if it was attacked. However, a secret part of the agreement stated that it only referred to an attack by Germany. The British government decided not to reveal this caveat, because everyone would want to know if there were any other secret diplomatic agreements.

By now the British government realised it could not help Poland stop the German attacks, never mind those made by the Soviet Union. Polish Ambassador Edward Raczyński asked British Foreign Secretary Edward Wood, Earl of Halifax, what Britain intended to do and was told it was up to the Prime Minister. He decided not to declare war on the Soviet Union. The British government was also looking to the future because it would want to trade with the Soviets if it faced a war with Germany. At best it was hoping that it could form an alliance with the Soviets. Meanwhile the French government thought the German-Soviet alliance would not last, so Prime Minister Édouard Daladier kept quiet. On 31 October, Molotov summarised that the double blows by the Wehrmacht and the Red Army were 'enough for nothing to be left of this bastard of the Treaty of Versailles'.

The defence of the eastern border was ignored by a communist Poland and it was 1989 before the brave exploits of the Border Defence Corps were recognised. Only then was Lieutenant Jan Bolbot posthumously awarded the Virtuti Militari, Poland's highest military decoration, for fighting the Soviets until the end.

The Aftermath

It is believed that over 65,000 Polish troops were killed in the month-long battle, compared to 16,000 German troops and maybe 1,500 Red Army soldiers (numbers vary widely). However, the rapid advances and fractured nature of the fighting meant that the Wehrmacht captured around 420,000 Polish soldiers while the Soviets took another 240,000 prisoners.

The Wehrmacht and the Red Army lost around 270 tanks between them while the Polish army lost 130, but it was a higher percentage of their total. Around 120,000 Polish troops escaped to neutral Romania, while another 20,000 headed north to Latvia and Lithuania. Many would escape to fight again from France and Britain.

One myth that persists from the invasion is that Polish cavalry fought German tanks. Around ten per cent of Polish soldiers were mounted but they were used as reconnaissance troops or fast moving infantry in the absence of lorries. They knew their weaknesses, and while they were supported by anti-tank rifles and guns, they always avoided German armour. But they were occasionally ambushed by tanks while they attacking infantry and a foreign journalist reported that Polish cavalry were charging German tanks on at least one of these occasions.

Most of the Polish Air Force's squadrons were relocated to small, camouflaged airfields before the Germans attacked, but their planes were obsolete and their pilots were outnumbered. Even so, the Luftwaffe had over 500 aircraft shot down or damaged. The Poles lost 333 aircraft, a far higher percentage of their strength.

The division of Polish territory into Gaue and the General Government.

Chapter 7

Establishing a Greater Reich

Implementing Nazi and Soviet policies

Occupying Poland

Military commanders and civil administrators were given interim control of four areas of Poland as the Wehrmacht advanced east in September 1939. Military and paramilitary units were deployed to maintain security, while German staff replaced their Polish counterparts in all levels of the administration. By mid-September, General Walter Heitz and Albert Forster had taken control of West Prussia in the north-west, while General Alfred von Vollard-Bockelberg and Arthur Greiser had taken the Posen Reich District in the west. Major General Gerd von Rundstedt and Hans Frank took control of the central area and Major General Wilhelm List and Arthur Seyss-Inquart installed themselves in the southern area. The temporary situation ended on 8 October when the west area of Poland, and its ten million people, were annexed to Germany. It was divided into four Reich districts or *Gaue*, and each one was run by a Gauleiter. German Christians were granted citizenship but Polish Christians and all Jews were denied it, making them stateless.

Gauleiter Albert Forster remained in control of the West Prussia Reich District but it was renamed the Danzig-West Prussia Reich District in January 1940. His views on Poland were made clear when he said that Germany had to 'exterminate this nation, starting from the cradle'. His men started with 12,000 members of the intelligentsia who were rounded up and murdered in the woods around Piaśnica, north-west of Gdynia. Around 65,000 inmates of Stutthof concentration camp, east of Danzig, would be murdered, worked to death or die from illness during the course of the war. The few Jews in Danzig and West Prussia were also held in the camp before they were taken to the extermination camps.

The Posen Reich District was renamed the Wartheland Reich District and was governed by Gauleiter SS-Obergruppenführer Arthur Greiser. SS and Police Leader SS-Gruppenführer Wilhelm Koppe organised the intelligentsia actions and then declared that he wanted to make Łódź 'free from Jews'. Koppe was involved in the early gassing experiments of patients at Soldau concentration camp and then at Chełmno extermination camp, starting in the autumn 1941.

The territories north of Warsaw were incorporated into the East Prussia Reich District under Reich Commissioner Erich Koch. The area west of Krakow became part of the Silesia Reich district under Josef Wagner but it would be split into Upper and Lower Silesia, under Fritz Bracht and Karl Hanke in 1941.

Hans Frank was promoted to rule the four Districts (Gaue) as well, making him supreme chief of all German occupied territories. The final part of the German plan for Poland was to make the central and southern parts into the General Government on 26 October and it was going to be treated very differently to the rest.

The eventual plan would be to remove the Poles and the Jews from the four districts to make way for ethnic Germans. The Polish elite were being murdered; ghettos would be established for the Jews and the rest would be moved into the General Government with a view to using them as slave labour. The four Gaue could then be populated with ethnic Germans with the General Government following on later.

The launch of Operation Barbarossa in June 1941 created new areas to administer and the Białystok area was attached to East Prussia in August. Reich Commissioner Hinrich Lohse took control of Reich Department Ostland, which covered north-east Poland and the Baltic States, at the same time. Reich Commissioner Erich Koch also took over Reich Department Ukraine which covered eastern Poland, while the General Government was extended to cover south-east Poland.

The same brutal Living Space (*Lebensraum*) policies were implemented across the new territories. Many Poles were deported, some were Germanised, and the rest were murdered. The Jewish communities had been increased by the many refugees escaping the German advance across Poland in the autumn of 1939. But there was no escape this time, and they were rounded up by the *Einsatzgruppen* and executed.

The General Government

A decree on 8 October 1939 declared that the ten million Polish nationals living in the central and southern areas of the country were stateless. A second decree stated that the General for the Occupied Polish Territories Government would take control of the area on 26 October; the name would be changed to the General Governorate on 31 July 1940. Hans Frank was appointed Governor-General of what was often referred to as the Remainder of Poland.

Frank located his government in Kraków (Krakau in German) because he considered Warsaw to be too dangerous. He was aided by his Chief of the Government, Josef Bühler, and his Chief of the Police, Friedrich-Wilhelm Krüger. SS-Obergruppenführer Koppe replaced Krüger after a dispute with Frank in October 1943 and the Warsaw concentration camp was just one of his many responsibilities. He soon became a target of Operation Heads and was injured during an assassination attempt in Kraków in July 1944.

The General Government was divided into four districts: Warsaw, Radom, Lublin and Kraków, but the Galicia district was added soon afterwards. It had fourteen ministries or departments: interior, justice, finance, economy, food, agriculture, labour, forestry, propaganda, education, science, construction, railways and post. Kraków and Galicia were merged into one district in March 1943, while Warsaw was divided into the Radom and Lublin districts. Steps were then taken to remove all the Poles from the Lublin district, to make way for German settlers, while Warsaw and Kraków became city districts.

Frank set about forcing the Jews into cramped ghettos and relocating Poles into inferior housing to make way for German settlers. Poles were evicted from the best accommodation to make way for the Germans, and their possessions were often seized. Eventually nearly one million Poles would be moved from the annexed areas into the General Government, to make way for a similar number of ethnic Germans. Tens of thousands would be held in Polish camps (*Polenlager*) before they were deported to the Reich to work, while the rest were put to work across the General Government. Those unfit for work were left to survive the best they could; four million would not.

Most of the cities, towns, villages and counties were given German names, while roads and other place names received the same treatment in September 1941. The state language was declared to be German but local government offices were still allowed to use Polish. Universities and high schools were closed down, because older children had to work, while younger children were taught the absolute minimum.

All Polish military officers were stripped of their rank, many were arrested and some were executed. Polish police personnel had to carry out basic duties such as manning checkpoints and helping the German Order Police with round-ups. It meant that Polish officers, nicknamed the Blue Police (so called because of the colour of their uniforms), were generally despised.

Frank ruled the General Government with an iron fist, sending Poles to work in Germany and cooperating with the transportation of the Jews to the extermination camps. Frank was at the top of the list of Nazi officers to be targeted under the Home Army's assassination campaign, and was under constant surveillance. However, he survived an attempt on his life when his train was derailed by partisans in January 1944.

Frank would be captured by American troops in Bavaria on 3 May 1945. He tried to blame everything on Heinrich Himmler and his SS and then failed to commit suicide when no one believed him. He converted to Roman Catholicism but he was still found guilty at the Nuremberg trials and was executed in October 1946.

Germanisation Plans

Hitler appointed Heinrich Himmler the Reich Commissioner for Strengthening the German Race in Occupied Territories on 7 October 1939. He coordinated the activities of the Main Welfare Office for Ethnic Germans and the Main Department of Race and Settlement as it planned and implemented the resettlement and extermination of Polish Christians and Jews. Over the next four and a half years he would issue orders which affected every Pole. The intelligentsia in Warthegau, South East Prussia and East Upper Silesia would either be killed or deported, while the rest of the Poles would be moved from Danzig-West Prussia into the General Government area. He also ordered the movement of all Jews into ghettos.

A directive at the beginning of 1940 instructed the Main Department of Race and Settlement to check Polish Christians for racial suitability. It was part of the plan to make rural areas German in five years, urban areas in ten years and the rest of the General Government after fifteen years. Racial Aliens, as he referred to them, would be means-tested and the acceptable would be included on the People's List (*Volksliste*) and then be subjected to tests to make them good German People (*Volksdeutsche*). Those on the Volksliste were taught how to behave as a German, while their children had to join the Hitler Youth and the German Girls League. They were forbidden from fraternising with the newcomers and those who refused to cooperate would be executed. Racially suitable young men and women could then be sent to Germany to work. Himmler issued a memorandum on what to do with Polish children in May 1940. Children deemed suitable for adoption would be sent to Germany, while the rest would only be given a basic education and would have to start manual work at a young age.

Gauleiters Albert Forster and Arthur Greiser would discover that only 1.7 million Poles were racially suitable, leaving 17 million people to be deported, and they were split into two categories. Special Cases (*Sonder-Fälle*) would be used as labour across what had been Poland, and the East Cases (*Ost-Fälle*), who would be gathered, ready to re-settle in captured areas to the east. The plan was to eventually deport those who were unfit to work to live in western Siberia.

The Central Bureau for Immigration would bring in 400,000 people from Germany and another 350,000 ethnic Germans from the Baltic States over the next three years. Members of the Hitler Youth and the German Girls League would help them settle in and their activities would then be monitored by the police.

Head of the Party Chancellery, Martin Bormann, said that the General Government would become 'a great Polish labour camp'. The Welfare Office for Ethnic Germans became part of the SS programme called the Strengthening of German Nationhood in 1942. It had already resettled hundreds of thousands of ethnic Germans into the Reich Districts of Danzig-West Prussia and Wartheland and cities in the General Government. Around 400,000 officials, technical staff, and clerks had been moved in from the *Altreich* (Old Reich) by 1938 to run them.

The Germans also set up the Ukrainian Committees in October 1939 to get their cooperation and to stir up anti-Polish sentiment. They helped the 30,000 Ukrainian refugees who had fled from Soviet controlled areas and negotiated the release of 85,000 prisoners of war taken by the Red Army. The Germans then supported Ukrainian economic and cultural activities, to get their support. They were also allowed to reopen churches, schools and theatres while a publishing house in Kraków printed books in Ukrainian.

General Plan East

The Nazi policy of Lebensraum demanded additional living space and extra resources for Germans. Studies had been made since the Nazis came to power in 1933 but General Plan East was eventually discussed in detail in the summer of 1940. It would involve the enslavement, expulsion and murder of fifteen million Poles over the next twenty years to make way for five million German settlers.

The German attack against the Soviet Union on 22 June 1941 changed the priorities concerning the movement of people in the East. Three proposals were tabled by the Reich Security Main Office to the Reich Ministry for the

Occupied Eastern Territories in 1942 and Himmler issued the final version of General Plan East on 29 October 1942.

The initial phase, called the Small Plan, called for the removal of most ethnic groups from German occupied areas before the end of the war. That included the murder of all Polish Jews and the execution or deportation to Siberia of many of the Polish Christians. The Big Plan called for the deportation or execution of 31 million people during the twenty-five years after the war. Another 14 million would be forced to work for the Germans. Only 3 to 4 million racially valuable Poles would be allowed to stay and they would be dispersed across Poland and become Germanised.

The eventual plan was to wipe out the ethnic Poles and General Plan East estimated that over 10 million of the slave labourers would die through overwork and malnutrition. The survivors would be forbidden to marry or cohabit, so that the Polish race would die out by the 1970s.

General Plan East was a short-term plan of annihilation of the Polish Jews but it was also a long-term plan to wipe out the Polish all together. But the plan was put on hold following the German defeat at Stalingrad in February 1943 and was soon abandoned altogether.

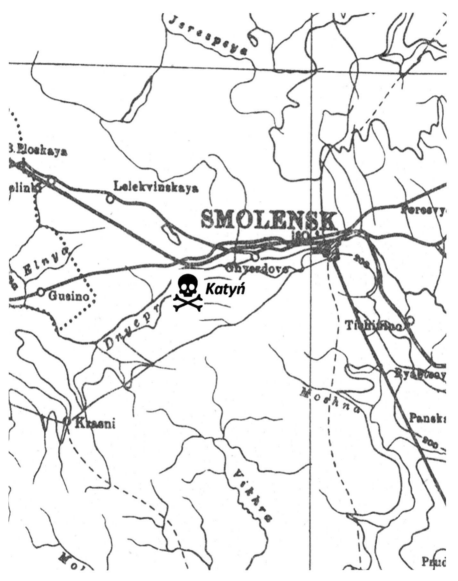

The location of Katyń, west of Smolensk.

Chapter 8

There Must be No Polish Leaders

Eliminating the Intelligentsia

The Security Services

The Germans introduced many layers of policing to maintain security. Ordinary policing duties were carried out by the German personnel of the Order Police (*Ordnungspolizei* or *OrPo*) and the Polish personnel of the Blue Police. They were often involved in deporting the Poles to the General Government, the relocation of Jews into ghettos, and the murderous actions against the intelligentsia. They carried out many atrocities during the course of their work.

The Security Police (*Sicherheitspolizei* or *SiPo*) was composed of the Criminal Police (*Kriminalpolizei* or *Kripo*) and the Gestapo and they were engaged in tracking down 'enemies of the state'. They were involved in Operation Tannenberg, the round-up and execution of Poland's intelligentsia identified before the war. They were then engaged in tracking down and executing the rest of the intelligentsia in the Extraordinary Pacification Actions in the spring and summer of 1940.

Hans Frank organised the Special Service (*Sonderdienst*) in May 1940 and around 3,000 ethnic Germans (*Volksdeutsche*) were formed into paramilitary units. They helped the police perform their many functions and often tracked down Poles who were providing support for Jews outside the ghetto.

An Auxiliary Police was formed from the People's Militia in the recently conquered Ukraine in August 1941 and the Germans played on their hatred for the Poles to get them to do the worse tasks. Mobile Protection Teams (*Schutzmannschaft* or *Schuma*) moved the Jews into ghettos and tracked down partisans, while the Ukrainian Police carried out typical policing duties.

The Gestapo and the Security Office

The Secret State Police (*Geheime Staatspolizei* or *Gestapo*) spent the autumn and winter of 1940 combing local authority registration records to identify the rest of the intelligentsia. The Gestapo targeted various organisations, including members of the National Democratic Party, the Red Cross, the Boy Scouts and local authority employees in 1941.

Suspects were arrested one-by-one, with raids being carried out by two or three officers, one of whom spoke Polish. Their car would pull up outside the target's address in the night. They made the doorman assure the tenants of the target apartment that he had to check something, like a faulty water valve. The Gestapo men would then rush in and violently cross-examine everyone inside before searching the property for evidence and valuables. The target, or hostages (usually family members) if they were absent, were then taken to the Gestapo headquarters. The hostages were either shot or sent to concentration camps if the target did not hand themselves in. The questioning that followed was accompanied with more violence and confessions and sometimes led to new investigations.

The Security Office or *Sicherheitsdienst* (SD) was an intelligence agency which ran a network of agents and informants searching for suspects. It dealt with the Church, the Jews and the press while the Gestapo dealt with Marxists, saboteurs and other enemies of the state. It controlled the *Einsatzgruppen* and often supplied personnel for their round-ups and executions. The SD later collected information on the Jewish ghettos, to help the Order Police maintain order and security.

Operational Groups

Einsatzgruppen or Operational Groups had already been used in Austria and Czechoslovakia, where they had taken control of government and police offices, seized documents and interrogated staff. However, their main task was to round up and execute potential enemies of the state. They had also been involved in the murder of incurable hospital patients under the secret T4 programme.

SS-Standartenführer Hans-Joachim Tesmer recruited suitable candidates from the SS, the Security Service, the police and the Gestapo for the groups. SS-Obergruppenführer Werner Best organised them into seven companies, each with around one hundred men, and they came under the Reich Main Security Office in September 1939.

The Operational Groups followed the Wehrmacht into towns and cities and rounded up the intelligentsia listed in the Gestapo's Special Investigation Book. They were carrying out Hitler's order that 'there must be no Polish leaders; where Polish leaders exist they must be killed, however harsh that sounds.'

Einsatzgruppe VI followed Third Army from East Prussia while Einsatzgruppe IV followed Fourth Army from West Prussia. Einsatzgruppe III, II and I trailed Eighth, Tenth and Fourteenth Armies across southwest Poland. Einsatzgruppe VI was deployed in central Poland while Einsatzgruppe VII worked across Silesia.

Order Police and military units were drafted in to help the *Einsatzgruppen* round up the intelligentsia during the Actions. The Self-Protection paramilitaries also helped during the executions and around 65,000 were murdered in just three months. The *Einsatzgruppen* then helped move the Jews into the city ghettos before they returned to their murderous anti-intelligentsia operations at the start of Operation Barbarossa in June 1941.

Self-Protection Units

Self-Protection units (*Selbstschutz*) had caused confusion behind the Polish army's lines during the invasion. Some sabotaged railways, some spread rumours, causing panic amongst the Polish civilians, while a few fired at passing units. Members often dressed in Polish uniforms to increase the confusion.

The SS soon took control of the 82,000 members but they became renowned for their unruly conduct, corruption and their brutal treatment of prisoners while they helped the *Einsatzgruppen*. The Self-Protection units were disbanded in November 1939, but some units continued to operate until the Actions were complete the following spring.

Nazi Ethnic Classification

The Germans viewed ethnicity according to a person's blood, attitude and religion. Everyone who lived in Poland was put into one of four categories: immigrant Germans, German People (*Volksdeutsche*), Poles and Jews.

The Germans who had relocated from Germany (the *Reichdeutsche*) were the highest-ranking citizens and they would be given the best of everything: housing, jobs, transport and facilities. Ethnic Germans had their names added to the People's List (the *Volksliste*). Some chose to go on the list so they would be treated better, while others had to join the list if they wanted to keep their house or job. They were classified into one of four categories: collaborators with Germany were category 1 or 2, according to how German they were; those who had remained neutral were category 3 or 4, for the same reason. Poles were assessed in a similar fashion, according to what extent their interviewers thought they could be Germanised. Gypsies and then Jews came at the bottom of the racial hierarchy.

One million Poles had been classified as ethnic Germans by the end of 1944 and Categories 1 and 2 had been moved onto middle-sized farms. Category 3 were initially sent to Germany to work, but they were made to work on small farms after January 1940. Category 4A (*Alt Reich* or Old Reich) were sent to Germany to work and Category 4S Poles (*Sonder-Fälle* or Special Cases) were moved to the General Government. People from other ethnic groups were deported to their homelands.

The Germans viewed the Poles as sub-humans and had no wish to mix with them, either professionally or socially. They intended to murder the educated ones, make the uneducated ones work hard, limit their children's schooling and control their reproduction. Poles were evicted from the best houses and apartments, sacked from good jobs and banned from making friends with Germans. Sexual relations were made illegal and while men could be deported for cohabiting, women could be forced to work in a brothel.

The Warsaw Prisons

The men's prison on Peacock Street (Pawiak Street) could hold several thousand prisoners and the Gestapo took it over in the autumn of 1939. Tens of thousands of political prisoners, partisans and hostages would be interrogated inside its walls. Around 37,000 people were killed, either in reprisal shootings or from torture, and another 60,000 were sent to labour camps or concentration camps. Governor Franz Bürkl was assassinated in September 1943 and twenty prisoners were shot in revenge.

Mokotów Prison was also used by the Gestapo and it was known as the 'place of no return'. Goose House on Goose Street (Gęsia Street) was a camp used to house Jews before they were deported. The Security Police and the Secret Service established their headquarters on Szucha Avenue. Thousands were interrogated inside its walls and many were killed; their ashes were later found in the cellars.

Most of the Pawiak prisoners were moved to concentration camps across Germany just before the Warsaw Uprising started on 1 August 1944. There was heavy fighting around the prison and the remaining prisoners were shot before they could be rescued. The complex was blown up when the uprising ended. Around 300 inmates were released from Mokotów Prison during the uprising, but the Germans executed the remaining

500 prisoners when they recaptured it. The scouts of the Zośka battalion used two captured Panther tanks to release 350 Jewish prisoners from the Goose House camp at the beginning of the uprising. Many fought and died alongside the Home Army.

The NKVD held German war criminals, members of the underground and political prisoners in the prisons during the last months of the war. The Polish Ministry of Public Security (MBP) then took it over after the war and the prison executioner Piotr Śmietański, nicknamed 'the Butcher', shot many in the basement boiler room.

The Murder of Hospital Patients

The Reich Medical Service had been murdering incurable hospital patients across Germany under the secret T-4 Euthanasia Programme since July 1939. The same activities started happening across Poland on 22 September 1939. A German director would take control of a psychiatric hospital, the patients would be assessed, and then the staff would be told they were being transferred to another facility. Instead they were either taken to an execution site and shot, or killed in sealed trucks which pumped carbon monoxide into the back. Over 15,000 patients and staff were murdered while another 10,000 patients died from hunger and neglect.

The Gestapo and NKVD Conferences

Despite their political differences, the Chief of the German Police, Heinrich Himmler, and the head of the NKVD, Lavrentiy Beria, had similar ideas on how to deal with Poland and the Poles. The Gestapo and the NKVD agreed to exchange soldiers and refugees, to deport civilians and to carry out mass executions during secret meetings held between September 1939 and March 1940. Having agreed they wanted to eliminate the Polish intelligentsia, the Germans implemented the Extraordinary Pacification Action (*AB Aktion*) and Special Action Krakau. The NKVD also began the interrogations of Polish officers which eventually led to the Katyń massacre.

Soviet Occupation of Poland

The Ribbentrop-Molotov Pact had agreed that the Red Army would invade Poland's eastern territories around two weeks after the German attack in the west. The need to safeguard the ethnic Belarusians and Ukrainians in the Kresy from the Poles was given as the excuse for the invasion.

The Germans attacked on 1 September and more than 330,000 Poles (many of them Jews) fled east to escape the fighting over the next two weeks. The Red Army then crossed the border on 17 September and resistance was minimal because the majority of the Polish army units had been moved west. The Soviet Union never declared war on Poland because Moscow claimed that the Polish state had ceased to exist by the time its troops crossed the border. The Red Army occupied around half of Poland, an area of over 77,000 square miles, and around six million Poles came under Moscow's control. Germany and the Soviet Union signed the Treaty of Friendship, Cooperation and Demarcation on 28 September. The northern part of the Kresy was given to Lithuania while the rest was divided between the Belorussian and Ukrainian Soviet Socialist Republics. The Soviets then set about implementing communist ideals across the occupied areas, starting with the conscription of over 200,000 men.

Moscow portrayed Poland as a capitalist state which exploited the working classes and the minorities, so it exploited ethnic tensions, by supporting the Lithuanians, Byelorussians and Ukrainians. Time and again the authorities incited violence to give the NKVD the excuse to round up or murder Poles. Some Poles, notably the Jews, thought the Soviets would look after them, but it was soon clear that everyone was a target.

The Soviets held an election on 22 October 1939 to legitimise the situation in eastern Poland and the result was in favour of the annexation. The voting had been rigged but it gave the Soviets the go-ahead to replace the Polish establishment with their own version. The Poles were made Soviet citizens and Lithuanian, Belarusian and Ukrainian were declared the official languages, ahead of Polish. The Soviets introduced communist policies by nationalising all previously state-owned property, redistributing private property and taking control of all industries. Agricultural land was seized and divided between the peasants, so collective farms could be formed. Equipment and labour were shared, to make it easier to reach the quotas set by the state. However, the Polish peasants were wary of the new system, because they were mindful of the famine which had devastated Soviet-controlled areas of Belorussia and the Ukraine in recent years.

Factories and hospitals were stripped of their equipment and it was distributed across the Soviet Union. Churches were shut, schools had to teach a communist curriculum, libraries were shut down and publishing houses were closed. Polish memorials and monuments were demolished, while place names and street names were changed. The economy was rigged in favour of Soviets by introducing the rouble at a rigged exchange rate to the złoty. Taxes were also raised and businesses were banned from raising their prices.

Every political party except the Communist Party was banned, local authority staff were replaced, and new laws and regulations were introduced. Schools and universities could only teach Soviet-approved subjects, so Polish history and culture were banned. Newspaper articles and radio items had to be approved by Moscow to follow the Party line. The Soviet rouble then replaced the złoty, just before Christmas, meaning that the Poles lost all their savings. All aspects of life were controlled by a restrictive police state and the NKVD interrogated or imprisoned anyone believed to be stepping out of line. Over 100,000 members of the intelligentsia, and others who had worked for the Polish state, would have been imprisoned or executed by the Nazis by June 1941.

The Soviet Union had not signed the Hague and Geneva conventions covering the treatment of prisoners of war. It referred to the 250,000 Polish soldiers who had surrendered to the Red Army rebels as being guilty of committing 'counter-revolutionary activity'. Other ranks were deported to one of the Gulag camps across the Soviet Union. The officers were interrogated by the NKVD to discover what their political views were, to decide their fate.

Over one million Polish men, women and children were deported across the Soviet Union over an eighteen-month period. Around 220,000 were sent to the far-east territories in February 1940 – they had to endure days and nights in slow moving railway wagons on the 6,000 mile journey across the frozen steppes; the next batch of 320,000 people were scattered across the vast Kazakhstan area in April 1940; a third group of 240,000 were shipped east in the summer of 1940; and the final 300,000 were deported just before Operation Barbarossa in June 1941.

In all, around 1.5 million Poles were sent to work as slave labourers across the Soviet Union and half were dead by the time the Sikorski-Mayski Agreement re-established diplomatic relations in July 1941. The Soviet Union released nearly 400,000 Polish men and while many were again conscripted into the Red Army, another 30,000 had to join General Berling's Polish Army, which served with the Red Army on the Eastern Front. Many were allowed to join new Polish military units but Stalin lost interest in the project because of a shortage of weapons and food, so they were allowed to leave the Soviet Union. Over 120,000 would be evacuated to Iran under General Władysław Anders and they joined the Allied fight across the Mediterranean.

The imprisonments, deportations and executions of the ethnic Poles of the Kresy equalled, if not exceeded, the horrors inflicted by the Germans. However, the Soviets would always remind the Poles of their version of history with the statement, 'be grateful because we freed you from Nazism.'

The NKVD Prison Massacres

By the early summer of 1941, the prisons across the Kresy were filled with ethnic Belarusians and Ukrainians who had fallen foul of the Soviet system. The launch of Operation Barbarossa on 22 June took the NKVD by surprise and many guards panicked. Around 45,000 prisoners were put on trains or made to march, but over 9,000 were murdered in the prisons, often in the most gruesome manner. For example, the guards of Łuck prison promised the prisoners they would be released if they did not try to escape after an air strike had demolished the wall. But they were then paraded in front of tanks and machine-gunned to death. Another 1,200 prisoners were burnt to death in Kharkiv prison because the guards had no time to evacuate them. The advancing Germans found hundreds of bodies, many of them mutilated, in the abandoned prisons. Only 3,500 shaken survivors had been left behind in the chaotic retreat.

Chapter 9

Fighting Back at Home

Resistance groups until the summer of 1943

Early Resistance Groups

Several partisan groups sprang up in the wake of the surrender of Poland and they were formed by army officers who had escaped capture. They followed political lines to begin with, but most settled their differences as the war dragged on and joined together to fight for a free Poland. They would eventually grow into the largest underground resistance movement in World War II.

The Political Consultative Committee maintained contact between the Polish resistance groups and the Government-in-Exile in London after February 1940. It was renamed the Government Delegation in December 1940, which marked the beginning of the Underground State. It then started supervising the creation of military and civilian administrations across the German and Soviet occupied territories.

Poland's Victory Service and the Armed Struggle Union

Commander General Michał Karaszewicz-Tokarzewski (codenamed the Doctor) formed Poland's Victory Service on 27 September 1939, while the Polish military prepared to surrender. It carried out the earliest partisan attacks and was renamed the Armed Struggle Union in November 1939. General Kazimierz Sosnkowski was nominally in charge, but he had limited control because he was based in France.

The Armed Struggle Union's operations were divided between the German and Soviet occupied zones in January 1940. Colonel Stefan Rowecki (codename Spearhead) ran anti-German operations from his headquarters in Warsaw while General Karaszewicz-Tokarzewski organised anti-Soviet operations from his headquarters in Lwów.

General Wladyslaw Sikorski had to relocate to London when France capitulated in June 1940 and he made Colonel Rowecki his deputy. He took over all operations across Polish territory after Karaszewicz-Tokarzewski was arrested by the NKVD. Karaszewicz-Tokarzewski was later released and he eventually became General Władysław Anders' deputy in the Polish army in the East.

Rowecki set up the Reprisal Union as the Armed Struggle Union's sabotage group in April 1940 and it was run by Lieutenant Franciszek Witaszek (codename Guard). His men attacked military facilities or factories until they joined the Directorate of Diversion (*KeDyw*), the Home Army's sabotage arm, in February 1942.

The Armed Struggle Union also carried out assassinations and the Austrian-born actor Igo Sym was one of their high priority targets during the early part of the war. He was director of Warsaw's State Theatre but he was also a Gestapo informant who even denounced his pre-war screen partner, actress Hanka Ordonówna. Sym was working on the film *Homecoming*, a propaganda film depicting the Polish suppression of ethnic Germans, when he was shot dead at his home on 7 March 1941. The reprisals were swift and harsh as over twenty hostages were executed, 120 people were arrested, and all the city theatres were closed.

Sabotage Units

The Armed Struggle Union brought together various sabotage units in April 1940 and then split them into Retaliation Union units, to avoid detection. Major Franciszek Niepokólczycki (codename Theodore) organised assassinations, intelligence gathering, propaganda, and attacks against military units. His group also specialised in carrying out reprisals following rounds-ups or executions.

The number of Retaliation Union units increased after General Władysław Sikorski lifted the restrictions on sabotage in February 1942 and they started blowing up supply deports, outposts, trains and railways. Colonel Antoni Chruściel (codename Fitter) scored a major victory when his men cut all the railway lines into Warsaw on the night of 7–8 October 1942, stopping all train movements for nearly twelve hours. However, eighty-nine inmates of the Pawiak prison were executed as punishment. The Retaliation Union units became part of the Diversion Directorate (*KeDyw*) in February 1943.

Lieutenant Colonel Jan Włodarkiewicz (codename Damien) formed several sabotage units after Barbarossa was launched in June 1941. The 'Eighteen' and then the 'Twenty-Seven' followed the German armies into the Soviet Union, attacking and spying along their supply lines.

The groups increased to around 1,000 members and Lieutenant Colonel Adam Grocholski (sometimes known as the Engineer) took over the partisan organisation which became known as the Fan (*Wachlarz*). One group was arrested in the winter of 1942-3 but Jan Piwnik (codename Grim) led the group of the Silent Unseen which released them from Pińsk prison while dressed in German uniforms. The Wachlarz units joined the KeDyw in March 1943.

Another group, called Vengeance, carried out partisan activities in Tarnobrzeg. The scouts and students were led by their school teacher Lieutenant Władysław Jasiński (codename Andrew, his son's name). The Little Andrews trained partisans, carried out sabotage and tried to free prisoners across central Poland. Jasiński was killed on 9 January 1943 and the Home Army welcomed Wiącek Sowa's members a couple of months later.

The Grey Ranks

The Polish Scouting and Guide Associations were banned by the Nazis and the Soviets, so Florian Marciniak (codename Nowak) formed an underground version on 27 September 1939. The headquarters was codenamed the Bee Yard and the scouts and guides were organised into standards (beehives), districts (swarms), troops (families) and squads (bees). They all pledged 'to safeguard the organisation's secrets, to obey orders and to never hesitate to sacrifice their lives'.

To begin with, members distributed propaganda leaflets mockingly signed SS; the signature was later expanded into *Szare Szeregi*, meaning the Grey Ranks. Boys were soon helping the adults with surveillance, sabotage and assassinations. Some girls carried messages or weapons while others worked as nurses in underground hospitals. Children as young as twelve were soon allowed to join and they were called the *Zawiszas* after the famous medieval Polish knight. They distributed leaflets, put up propaganda posters, defaced Nazi and Soviet notices and painted resistance symbols. Aleksander Kamiński (codename Dąbrowski) organised a famous campaign called 'We will avenge Wawer' (*Pomścimy Wawer*) following a massacre in the Warsaw district at Christmas 1940. The letters 'P and W' also came to mean Fighting Poland (*Polska Walcząca*) and Anna Smoleńska adapted the symbol into a P connected with an anchor and it was called the *Kotwica*. She would die in Auschwitz, aged only 23, but her symbol lives on as a symbol of Polish resistance.

Tadeusz Zawadzki (codename Zośka) became known as the 'Anchor Man' because he painted the largest number of anchors in his district. He became even more well-known after rescuing troop leaders Jan Bytnar and

Henryk Ostrowski from a Gestapo prison van on 26 March 1943. Bytnar died of his injuries but Zawadzki learnt who their interrogators were from Ostrowski and they were assassinated. Zośka was killed during a raid on a border post on 21 August 1943.

Stanisław Broniewski (codename Stefan Orsza and Witold) took command of the Grey Ranks in May 1943 and he oversaw the expansion of the organisation to over 8,000 members while secret training allowed members to play a bigger role in sabotage attacks. They were involved in Operation WISS which involved watching military units, while sabotage missions became more effective, prison breaks became bolder and assassinations more numerous.

The youngsters continued to hand out news sheets to the Poles and made sure the German soldiers saw their propaganda leaflets. They ripped down Nazi flags and posters and painted 'only for Germans' on lampposts because they wanted to see them hanging from them. The Grey Ranks was disbanded in January 1945, at the same time as the Home Army, to avoid its members being targeted by the NKVD.

The Silent Unseen (*Cichociemni*), 1941 to 1943

Polish officers Jan Górski and Maciej Kalenkiewicz (codename Kotwicz) had escaped to France in the autumn of 1939 and then to Britain in the summer of 1940. They convinced General Władysław Sikorski to form a Special Forces unit which could be deployed to Poland. The British Special Operations Executive trained over 2,600 soldiers to use weapons, explosives and mines. They were also taught a range of covert skills, practised unarmed combat and learned about life in occupied Poland. Only 600 passed and they were sworn into the Silent Unseen and given a new identity.

Dozens were parachuted into Poland with arms and supplies, starting in February 1941, and they joined the Reprisal Union's sabotage units. Some were even parachuted into France to start an underground movement among the half million strong Polish ex-pat community.

Other Resistance Groups

Lieutenant Colonel Jan Włodarkiewicz, Captain Witold Pilecki (codenames included Companion) and Władysław Surmacki (codename Stefan) formed the Secret Polish Army in central Poland in November 1939. The number of members soon rose to around 19,000, many of them ex-soldiers armed with the guns they had hidden following the September invasion. The two officers would soon merge their partisan organisation with the Armed Struggle Union.

Surmacki and Pilecki made sure they were arrested in Warsaw in September 1940, with a view to finding out what was happening to those being taken away during the round-ups. They were sent to Auschwitz, west of Kraków, where Pilecki organised a resistance group called the Military Organisation Union while Surmacki collected information about conditions in the camp. Their findings were smuggled to the Armed Struggle Union's headquarters the following spring. The information would be forwarded to the Government-in-Exile and they in turn informed the Allied governments of the harsh conditions in the camp.

Poland's three right-wing parties formed underground movements in October 1939. The National Party formed the National Army, but it had soon changed its name to the National Military Organisation. It would grow to have 80,000 members but had lost power because the Gestapo arrested many supporters of the National Party over the winter of 1940-41. Some members then merged with the Home Army in the spring of 1942, while the rest concentrated on capturing collaborators working for the Germans.

The National Radical Camp ABC (named after its newspaper) transformed into the Rampart Union underground movement in the autumn of 1939. Its military arm was the Lizard Union (named after a medieval order of knights) and it carried out sabotage and assassination missions. The National Radical Camp Falanga (or phalanx) formed the Confederation of the Nation in 1940 but it never had many members and eventually merged with the Armed Struggle Union.

Many soldiers hid in the forests and organised themselves into partisan groups. The Forest People (*Leśni*), as they became known, attacked army posts, military convoys and railway tracks. Occasionally they attacked German units and Major Henryk Dobrzański's (codename Hubal) group decimated an infantry battalion in March 1940. Some of the Forest People were encouraged to join Poland's Victory Service or the Armed Struggle Union but others, like the Pomeranian Union, preferred to remain independent and their numbers grew into thousands as the war dragged on.

Students formed a National Alliance in south-east Poland when the Soviets invaded in September 1939. They rose up in Czortków in January 1940 when Red Army units started leaving the town, in what was the first Polish uprising of the war. But they had insufficient weapons and while several dozen were arrested, twenty-four of the students would be executed in the Katyń massacre.

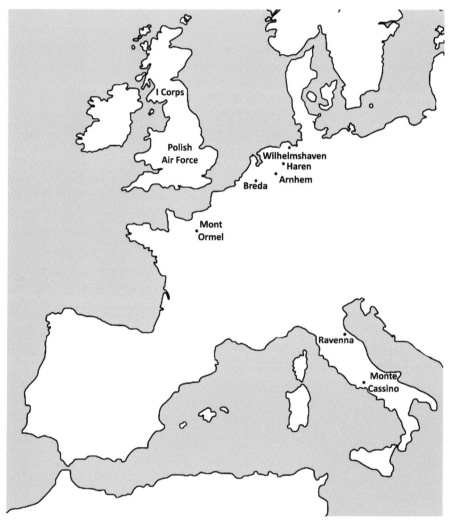

The areas of operation of Polish soldiers and airmen across Europe.

Chapter 10

Fighting Back from Abroad

Poland's Free Forces in exile

The Polish Free Forces

After the surrender of Poland, many Polish soldiers, seamen and airmen escaped, some directly to Britain and some via France. Others were captured and then released by the Soviet Union. They were all desperate to fight back against the invaders of their country and so a Polish Army, Navy and Air Force were organised. They would play significant roles in the defeating of the Third Reich, on the ground, at sea and in the air.

The Government-in-Exile

The President of the Polish Republic, Ignacy Mościcki, appointed Władysław Raczkiewicz as his successor after the Red Army invaded Poland, and Raczkiewicz would be appointed the President of the Republic in Paris after Poland surrendered. A plan was then made to establish a government to guide affairs in occupied Poland, even though German and Soviet troops were now installed across the country.

The ruling council was originally called the Government of the Republic of Poland in Exile, and it had General Władysław Sikorski as its prime minister and commander-in-chief of all the Polish armed forces still able to fight. It moved from Paris to Angers and finally to England after France fell in June 1940. It would often be referred to as the London government. Sikorski had been ignored in Poland for several years, but the saying 'Sikorski is nearer when the sun is higher' reflected the widespread support which stemmed from his charismatic personality.

The Government-in-Exile was a coalition council with members from several of Poland's political parties, and the Western Allied governments would work with it. It stayed in contact with the underground operating in Poland, giving advice and direction on how to be effective. The Government-in-Exile established diplomatic relations with the Soviet Union when Operation Barbarossa began in June 1941. Moscow agreed to free thousands of Poles who had been deported across the Soviet Union. General Władysław Anders gathered enough soldiers to form eight military divisions and they made a long and difficult journey through Iran to the Middle East. The Polish II Corps would join the Allied fight across the Mediterranean.

The Government-in-Exile's Ministry of Information published three books outlining atrocities inflicted on the people of Poland between 1940 and 1942. The White Book covered the crimes committed before the war, while the Black book documented the atrocities carried out against the Poles in the aftermath of the invasion. Jan Karski delivered an account of the Jewish Holocaust to the Government-in-Exile, the first report that the Germans were pursuing a policy of extermination against the Jews. Foreign Minister Count Edward Raczyński passed on the information to the governments of the United Nations in December 1942 and the material was included in a third volume.

The Germans told the world that they had discovered a mass grave of Polish officers in Katyń Wood in April 1943, hoping to cause problems between the Allies. Moscow denied they had been shot by the Red Army while the evidence strongly suggested they had. The Western Allies were prepared to accept Stalin's explanation to maintain the alliance. But the Government-in-Exile refused to believe the Soviets and so Moscow ended diplomatic relations with the Poles.

The Government-in-Exile was struck a serious blow when General Sikorski was killed when his plane crashed at Gibraltar in July 1943. The investigation reported an accident, but the Poles were convinced their leader had been assassinated. Stanisław Mikołajczyk took over but he did not have the same charisma as his predecessor and failed to get Stalin to discuss Poland's future, so he resigned in November 1944.

Mikołajczyk travelled to Poland to join the new Provisional Government of National Unity, believing that it was an honest attempt to set up a post-war government. However, the members were intent on establishing Communist rule and they won a rigged election in 1947. Mikołajczyk left Poland, fearing for his life, but the Western Allies decided to support the new administration. The British and the Americans decided it was time to remove their support for the Government-in-Exile, and the Polish Armed Forces in Exile were disbanded around the same time.

The Government at Home

The underground state formed the Political Consultative Committee to act as its government in Poland in February 1940. It had a cross-party membership which gave the Armed Struggle Union and then the Home

Army direction in their struggle with the Germans and the Soviets. The underground government was renamed the Home Political Representation in March 1943. It was again changed to the National Unity Council, in response to the new communist-controlled State National Council.

Kazimierz Pużak (codename Basil) issued a manifesto called 'Why Does Poland Fight?' in March 1944 and it had six main points. It wanted:

1. An independent, strong and safe Poland.
2. To defeat Nazi Germany and to make it rebuild the country.
3. To put all war criminals on trial.
4. To form alliances with the Western allies.
5. To restore diplomatic relations with the Soviet Union.
6. To restore the pre-war borders.

The Council asked the western powers for assistance in the Warsaw Uprising after the Red Army refused to help, but little could be done. It then complained that Poland was not invited to the Yalta Conference in February 1945, where Roosevelt, Stalin and Churchill discussed its post-war situation.

The advance of the Red Army across Poland then raised more pressing issues, as it arrested members of the Home Army. The Council stayed underground but most were arrested by the NKVD in March 1945 and taken to Moscow. They were questioned and accused in what became known as the 'Trial of the Sixteen'; three were acquitted, the rest were sentenced to time in prison, three died in captivity.

The National Unity Council reformed with new members in May 1945 and two months later it made several demands 'To the Polish Nation and the United Nations'. It wanted:

1. The Red Army to withdraw from Poland.
2. A return to democracy in Poland.
3. Social reforms introduced across the nation.
4. An end to reprisals against the Polish people.

The National Unity Council then dissolved and all of its demands were ignored.

The Polish Armed Forces in France

Sikorski started gathering those who had escaped to France and the ex-pats who were willing to fight together in the autumn of 1939. By June 1940 he had nearly 85,000 men but his plans to form four infantry divisions and independent infantry, and motorised and armoured brigades failed because of insufficient French support. Sikorski was also annoyed that the French high command had ignored his report assessing the blitzkrieg against Poland.

He only had two partially equipped infantry divisions and two independent brigades ready by the time the Germans attacked in May 1940. General Zygmunt Bohusz-Szyszko's Highland Brigade was the first to see action, at Narvik, in Norway. It returned to France just in time to defend Brittany, after which some escaped to England, the rest joined the French resistance.

The rest of the Polish troops were engaged in eastern France. The 1st Grenadier Division fought around Lagarde, in Lorraine, until General Bolesław Duch disbanded it on 21 June, but ships evacuated many to Britain, to fight another day. Brigadier General Prugar-Kietling's 2nd Fusiliers Division found itself surrounded near Belfort because the French had fallen back on its flanks, but many of the men broke out and escaped to Switzerland, where they were held in camps. The 10th Armoured Cavalry Brigade fought north-west of Dijon until it ran out of fuel, and then General Stanisław Maczek told his men to destroy their tanks and escape. The 4th Division had been left short of weapons, so all its men could do was flee to the coast and wait to be picked up. Marshal Philippe Pétain had replaced Paul Reynaud as Prime Minister on 16 June but the Poles ignored his calls to stop fighting. Three days later, Sikorski told all Polish units to head to the ports and wait to be evacuated to Britain or to cross the Swiss frontier.

In just five weeks, 1,400 Polish troops had been killed while another 4,000 had been wounded. Around 16,000 were taken prisoner by the Germans and another 13,000 were interned in Switzerland, but around 35,000 had reached Britain. The rest had gone into hiding and they would spend the next four years fighting as partisans, sometimes with the French resistance and sometimes on their own.

Many Polish pilots and their ground crews had also escaped to Romania and Hungary during the attack on Poland. Nearly 7,000 then transferred to France, where they found that they were going to be attached to French squadrons. The only all-Polish fighter squadron was the Groupe de Chasse Polonaise I/145 Warsaw and it was equipped with obsolete Caudron C714 fighters; another sixteen flights flew Morane-Saulnier MS406 fighters with French squadrons. Only 800 members of the Polish Air Force would see active service in France, due to a lack of planes.

Polish pilots flew over 700 sorties and shot down over fifty planes for the loss of 44 of their own. Most of the pilots and ground crew were evacuated to England, where they would play an important part in the Battle of Britain and later air battles.

Some Polish soldiers escaped to Britain or Switzerland while others were taken prisoner and were either given the choice of serving in the German armed forces or being held in a prisoner of war camp. Most of the Poles who had lived in France for some time went into hiding to avoid being arrested. General Aleksander Kawałkowski (codename Justyn) organised a Polish resistance movement in September 1941 to carry out sabotage, collect intelligence and distribute propaganda across France. They also gave assistance to thousands of Poles who had deserted from the Wehrmacht or the Nazi construction company Organisation Todt. Some would join their ranks and membership eventually peaked at around 4,000 members.

Members of the Silent Unseen were also parachuted into France to help, as were weapons, equipment and money. Then Colonel Daniel Zdrojewski was sent to take command of the Struggle for Polish Independence in July 1943 to work alongside the commander in chief of the French Interior Forces (FFI), General Marie-Pierre Koenig. The Polish partisans continued their sabotage and intelligence missions until the Allies freed France in the summer of 1944.

The Polish Air Force

On 18 June 1940, Prime Minister Winston Churchill declared 'the battle of France is over; the battle of Britain is about to begin.' Many Polish airmen and ground crews had escaped across the Channel and General Sikorski offered their services in the upcoming fight against the Luftwaffe. Air Chief Marshal Cyril Newall welcomed the offer of experienced reinforcements to the Royal Air Force but there were several conditions. They had to swear two oaths: one to the Polish government and another to King George VI. They would join the Royal Air Force Volunteer Reserve as pilot officers, the lowest rank, and they had to learn enough English to re-train in RAF procedures. They also had to wear British uniforms, fly in planes displaying British markings, and work alongside a British pilot to begin with. General Sikorski was told also that Poland would be charged for the costs of maintaining the Polish squadrons when the war was over.

The first four squadrons were formed in the summer of 1940, in time for the Battle of Britain. A total of 145 Polish fighter pilots would serve, the largest non-British contribution, and while they were experienced and fearless they were sometimes considered to be reckless. Over half flew in

British RAF squadrons until more squadrons were formed and there would be fourteen flying from British airfields by the spring of 1944. Polish Air Forces then came under Polish command,which had its own staff college.

There were four bomber squadrons. Number 300 (Masovia) Squadron and Number 301 (Pomerania) Squadron started with Fairey Battles in July 1940 but were switched to heavier Halifax bombers in the autumn. Number 300 Squadron was re-equipped with Avro Lancasters in March 1944. Number 304 (Silesia) Squadron was formed in August 1940 with Fairey Battles. But it flew Vickers Wellingtons for most of the war, as it carried out missions for Coastal Command. Number 305 (Greater Poland) Squadron briefly flew the Fairey Battle until Wellington bombers became available in November 1940. It would switch to the faster de Havilland Mosquitoes in December 1943.

There were twelve fighter squadrons. Number 302 (City of Poznan) Squadron was formed with Hawker Hurricanes in July 1940 and it was upgraded to Supermarine Spitfires in October 1941. Number 303 (Kosciuszko) Squadron started in August 1940 with Hurricanes and it would become the highest scoring squadron during the Battle of Britain, claiming 126 planes shot down. It was upgraded to Spitfires in January 1941 and then to North American Mustangs just before the end of the war. Number 307 (City of Lwów) Squadron was also formed in August 1940; it flew with Boulton Paul Defiants on night fighter missions. It switched to Bristol Beaufighters in August 1941 before flying Mosquitoes at the end of 1942.

Number 306 (City of Torun) Squadron and Number 315 (City of Deblin) Squadron began flying Hurricanes in September 1940. They switched to Spitfires in July 1941 and then Mustangs in March 1944. Number 308 (City of Krakow) Squadron was formed with Hurricanes in October 1940; it was upgraded to Spitfires in May 1941. Number 316 (City of Warsaw) Squadron and Number 317 (City of Wilno) Squadron operated Hurricanes from February 1941 and then Spitfires after October. Number 317 Squadron was given Mustangs in April 1944. The Polish Fighting Team flew Spitfires in North Africa between March and May 1943, to gain experience operating in close support. They were nicknamed Skalski's Circus after their squadron leader Stanisław Skalski.

There were two reconnaissance squadrons. Number 309 (Czerwien) Squadron formed in November 1940. Its flights were split up and they flew Westland Lysanders and North American Mustangs until Hurricanes became available in July 1944. Number 318 (City of Gdańsk) Squadron started with Hurricanes in April 1943 and was upgraded to Spitfires in March 1944.

Number 663 Squadron would form in Italy in October 1944 and it flew Auster liaison planes in an artillery observation role.

By the end of the war, 19,400 Poles were serving in Polish Air Force squadrons and other RAF squadrons. Fighter pilots had flown over 73,000 combat missions, destroying or damaging over 1,000 enemy planes; another 177 were probably kills. Bomber crews had flown over 11,700 sorties, dropping over 28,000 tons of bombs.

The Polish Navy

The Polish Navy had sent three destroyers to Britain just before the start of the war, under Operation Peking. The rest of its vessels were captured or destroyed but many sailors escaped to France and then Britain. The Royal Navy leased ships so Polish sailors who had no vessel could serve at sea. The cruiser HMS *Dragon* became ORP *Dragon* when it was handed over in January 1943; it was irreparably damaged by a mine off the coast of Normandy in July 1944. The cruiser HMS *Danae* was then handed over and renamed ORP *Conrad*, but it saw little action due to mechanical problems. The Poles also leased seven destroyers, three submarines and several other small vessels.

All three of the original Polish destroyers served during the Norwegian campaign in April 1940 but *Thunderbolt* was sunk during an aerial bombing attack, with the loss of one third of her crew. The remaining two ships then supported the vessels carrying the Dunkirk evacuation the following month. This time it was *Storm*'s turn to be hit during an air attack, on 24 May. The ship then served on convoy duty until it was turned into a training vessel in 1945; it ended the war as a submarine tender. *Lightning* survived the two operations unscathed to serve the rest of the war on convoy and patrol duties. It is remembered in Cowes, on the Isle of Wight, for driving off German bombers on the night of 4–5 May 1942; it also laid smoke to hide the town and its shipyard during the bombing raid.

The I Polish Corps

Around 6,000 Polish soldiers of the 4th Infantry Division were evacuated from La Pallice, near La Rochelle, in June and the division was rebuilt in Scotland. They would protect the coast until the end of the war. The rest of the soldiers who escaped France were organised by General Marian Kukiel's I Corps' headquarters into two fully manned brigades and five cadre brigades in September 1940. It had gathered around 14,000 men by the end of the year and one regiment had been armed with tanks and turned into the 10th Armoured Brigade. The 1st Tank Regiment expanded into the 16th Armoured Brigade and 2nd Infantry Regiment was reorganised as the 1st Independent Parachute Brigade in the autumn. A training brigade was also organised at the end of the year.

The 1st Armoured Division was formed the following spring and all the Polish troops were brought together under the renamed I Polish Armoured-Mechanised Corps. The corps acquired a new commander soon afterwards, General Mieczysław Boruta-Spiechowicz, and it completed training for the invasion of Nazi-occupied Europe while guarding the Scottish coastline.

The 1st Armoured Division was commanded by General Stanisław Maczek and was attached to the First Canadian Army in Normandy at the end of July 1944. The 'Black Devils', as they were known, were involved in Operation Totalize, starting on 8 August, and they were engaged in heavy fighting for Chambois and Mont Ormel. They then fought a fierce battle in their Sherman and Cromwell tanks to stop the Germans escaping from the Falaise Pocket, as part of Operation Tractable.

The 1st Armoured Division advanced along France and Belgium's north coast, reaching Breda in Holland soon after the Germans had fled. After a few quiet months following the failure of Operation Market Garden, the division moved along the Dutch-German border at the beginning of 1945. It crossed into Germany in April and reached Wilhelmshaven on Germany's northern coast on 6 May. General Maczek accepted the surrender of the East Frisian Fleet and ten infantry divisions around the naval base.

Major General Stanisław Sosabowski commanded the 1st Parachute Brigade; his original plan was to prepare for an air drop into occupied Poland to help the underground. The British government convinced the Poles to support the Normandy campaign instead but so many operations were cancelled that they asked to be dropped into Warsaw during the August 1944 uprising. That request was also turned down because it was considered too difficult, and the 1st Parachute Brigade landed in Holland as part of Operation Market Garden instead. Only a few Poles made it across the Rhine, into 1st British Airborne Division's bridgehead, but their actions did assist the evacuation across the river.

The 16th Armoured Brigade spent some time with the 1st Armoured Division but it was never deployed to the Continent. All the Polish troops in Germany assembled under I Corps when the war ended and they were engaged on occupation duties until they were disbanded in June 1947.

The II Polish Corps or Anders' Army

The Soviet Union and the Polish Government-in-Exile restored diplomatic relations in July 1941, in response to Operation Barbarossa. Thousands of Polish prisoners-of-war were released and assembled in southern Russia, under General Michał Tokarzewski. Initially 25,000 soldiers were formed into three infantry divisions and the Soviets wanted to deploy them on the Eastern Front. They all moved to Uzbekistan in the spring of 1942 and while a fourth division was formed it was clear that there was a shortage of officers. Moscow assured Anders that they were being transported from Siberia and other far flung camps across the Soviet Union, but they had all been executed in the Katyń massacre.

After Stalin lost interest in Anders' Army in March 1942, he let all 79,000 soldiers and 37,000 civilians head for British controlled territory. Many sailed across the Caspian Sea to Iran, while the rest endured a harsh cross-country march, through Iraq, eventually joining British Middle East Command in Palestine, where they became part of the Polish II Corps. Most of the Jews then transferred to British units to escape the anti-Semitic sentiments they had experienced on the long march.

Anders' Army fought in the Italian Campaign, participating in Eighth Army's final attack against Monte Cassino in May 1944. They suffered 3,800 casualties in one week but they convinced the Germans to withdraw from the hill-top monastery and a Polish flag was raised over the ruins. Their next battle was the attack on the Gothic Line, codenamed Operation Olive, where the Poles advanced along Italy's east coast, making a breakthrough towards Rimini in August 1944.

Anders' Army received over 10,000 reinforcements over the winter, the majority of them released prisoners from the Battle for Normandy who had been forced to fight for the Wehrmacht. They participated in the final Italian battle in April 1945, codenamed Operation Grapeshot, and broke through the German line west of Ravenna.

Despite his successful contribution to the Allies' war effort, the Polish communists stripped General Anders of his rank. He was not allowed to return to Poland and lived the rest of his life in England; he would be buried with his men in the Polish cemetery next to Cassino Monastery. A democratic Poland posthumously restored his rank and citizenship in 1989.

The main labour camps across occupied Poland; the shaded area shows the German Gaue.

Chapter 11

A Great Polish Labour Camp

The repression and elimination of Polish Catholics

Dividing Society

The Poles were forbidden from speaking Polish in the annexed districts and banned from speaking it in public places in the General Government. German had to be used in all offices and institutions, making it difficult to pay bills or sort out other day-to-day issues. It was also used on all official paperwork and approved translators were in great demand and at a high cost. All mail sent from prisons and other jails had to be written in German, which meant that most prisoners were unable to write to their relatives. All children were taught to speak basic German in school, but they were only shown how to write their name.

Access to public facilities was limited and Poles had to use separate cafés and restaurants, cinemas and theatres, parks and playgrounds. Signs said that Poles, Jews and dogs were not allowed to use public areas. Poles were also restricted in what buses and trams they could use, and they had to step aside and bow when they met a German on a footpath.

The Jews were at the bottom of the hierarchy. The Germans had no desire to mix with them and wanted to remove them entirely from society. To begin with, a long list of laws was introduced to isolate them economically. They were banned from owning businesses, having bank accounts or savings, working in certain professions or from using any public transport. They had to register their details and then, when the time came, they were forced into crowded ghettos. The final step for Poland's Jews was a train journey in a cattle car to an extermination camp.

The Judicial System

The Germans introduced a racist legal system which gave the Poles little protection, while the Jews had none. Military tribunals operated until a two-tier court system was introduced in June 1940. Polish courts dealt with standard criminal cases while special courts heard politically motivated crimes. Both types preferred to hand out corporal punishment rather than long prison sentences, because it had an immediate result. The guilty could be sentenced to hard labour, whipping, or execution. Most punishments were carried out in the prisons, but some were carried out in public places to set an example.

Religious Discrimination

The Catholic Church had encouraged the Poles living in Germany to speak out against the authoritarian regime before the war, so the Nazis exacted their revenge in the annexed areas. The head of the German bishops, Archbishop Adolf Bertram, asked the Vatican for permission to Germanise the Polish Church and Pope Pius XII agreed.

The Polish clergy were targeted under the intelligentsia actions and many priests were executed or held in concentration camps, while some went into hiding; altogether over 2,800 Polish clergy lost their lives during the war. German troops often desecrated churches, smashed or robbed religious items and burnt religious books. Many churches, monasteries and convents were closed or were turned into store houses and stables. Some church buildings were handed over to the Protestant United Evangelical Church, while a few were demolished.

A few churches stayed open, but they had to abide by strict rules or face being closed. All Polish signs on church property were replaced by German ones, German had to be spoken during masses, and the singing of patriotic hymns was banned. Only close family members could attend funerals, to stop them becoming focal points for protests. Attendances were high to begin with, as the people sought solace in their religion, but they soon dwindled because the police often rounded up the congregation at the end of a mass.

The Reich Minister of Church Affairs, Hanns Kerrl, took over church activities in Danzig-West Prussia, but Arthur was determined to close them all down across Wartheland. He reduced the United Evangelical Church to a civic association, so it lost its status in society.

Education and Culture

The Germans wanted to use Polish people as their slave labour and that included the workforce of the future. Schools for children over ten years old were closed while younger children were only taught the basics, such as counting and the writing of one's name; reading was banned. Classes were often cancelled while the children carried out manual tasks, such as snow clearing. The Germans were also determined to eliminate Polish culture and subjects like history, geography and literature were banned. Libraries were closed and their books burnt while other cultural centres, including theatres and music halls, were also shut down. Only the children who were taken from their Polish parents for adoption in Germany would receive a higher education.

Adults and teenagers were banned from learning manufacturing skills, trades and crafts, because they were reserved for Germans. Many teachers had been imprisoned or executed during the early actions, but the survivors set up the Secret Teaching Organisation to educate children. Many became involved in underground activities, along with their older pupils, joining the likes of the Grey Ranks and then the Home Army when they were older.

Economic Discrimination

The Bank of Poland had sent most of its assets abroad before the invasion and its seventy-five-ton gold reserve ended up in England and Canada. But the Germans did everything in their power to take control of the Polish economy, by setting the exchange rate at two złoty to one Reichsmark across the annexed territories; the black-market rate was higher for rationed goods. The rate favoured the German currency and the surplus helped finance the German economy; around 5.5 billion Reichsmarks had been transferred to the Wehrmacht by the start of 1945.

Poles were sacked from executive positions, to make way for German employees. Instead they had to do manual work for a low rate of pay for long hours without overtime payments. They had to pay higher taxes and contributions than the Germans and were banned from taking any holidays. The rules applied to any Poles over the age of 14 and any Jews over the age of 12.

The Germans confiscated state property, factories and large estates while anything else of value was seized and sometimes shipped across the Reich. All the Polish banks and credit institutions were closed across the General Government in 1940 while all assets were seized, so everyone lost their savings. Reich Credit Offices issued temporary bonds for the German controlled Bank of Issue, which was headed by the Polish economist Feliks Młynarski in December. A new currency, called the Kraków złoty, was then introduced but it had no backing and prices rose as inflation spiralled across the General Government. But Młynarski was also secretly working for the underground and his staff produced fake bank notes to undermine the German controlled economy. They also printed a range of documents in secret for the Home Army.

Eliminating the Polish Race

The Nazis wanted ethnic Germans from around the world to live together in the new 'Living Space' which had been Poland. The Poles would be moved into the General Government before they were scattered across the Reich or occupied territories to work as slave labourers. The Jews would be taken from their ghettos to the extermination camps. The annexed areas could then be repopulated with ethnic Germans.

The Ribbentrop-Molotov Pact called for the exchange of ethnic Germans and ethnic Russians between German and Soviet occupied areas. Negative Nazi propaganda about communism convinced tens of thousands of ethnic Germans to emigrate. Ships took people from the Baltic States while trains transported them from other territories. Personal belongings and small items were forwarded to their new homes, while larger items were sold off. The government kept the money raised and promised to give the refugees money as compensation. Plans to keep the economy stable by moving the required number of tradesmen and workers to each area often failed.

The refugees were evaluated on their arrival and those classified as Old Reich (*Altreich*) were settled in pre-1938 Germany. East Cases (*Ost-Fälle*) were settled in the annexed areas, which had once been Austria, Czechoslovakia and Poland. Special Cases (*Sonder-Fälle*) would be sent to the eastern territories the Nazis planned to conquer.

The Nazis' short-term plan was to murder the Jews in extermination camps, but they also introduced laws designed to reduce and eventually eradicate the Polish population. Polish men had to wait until they were 28 years old before they could marry, women had to wait until they were 25. The state provided no childcare for Polish children, and heating and food allowances were much lower for Polish families. It meant that fewer children would be born and infant mortality rates would be higher.

Married couples were kept separated while they worked in Germany and it was also illegal to have children out of wedlock. One of two things could happen to a Polish woman found to be pregnant in Germany: those deemed to be acceptable parents could have their child, but many women had to work right up to the birth, resulting in a high number of miscarriages;

the rest were forced to have an abortion. The new-born child could be given to a *Lebensborn* (Fountain of Life) institution, the SS-run clinics for racially acceptable children, ready to be adopted by a German family. The rest were placed in a Foreign Children Nursery while their mothers went back to work; many babies died through neglect or malnourishment.

Round-ups and Actions

An Action (*Aktion*) was the German name for a pre-planned or arbitrary round-up (called a łapanka by the Poles) of people. Some people were arrested because they had come to the attention of the Gestapo and they were imprisoned before they were taken to secret locations to be shot. Sometimes an action seized hostages following partisan activity and they would only be released if the perpetrators were captured or handed in. Round-ups were sometimes used to recruit people for manual labour, such as removing snow or rubble from the streets. But the people taken during an Action were often deported, either to work across the Reich or to build defensive positions in the East. Actions were also used to force Jews from their homes into ghettos or into work camps.

The earliest form of punishment was directed at the inhabitants of towns and villages around areas where the Polish army fought. The Wehrmacht announced it would shoot the people and burn their houses down, so Polish soldiers avoided built-up areas while the inhabitants were frightened of helping them. Nearly 9,000 people were executed as a result of the directive.

The first nation-wide action was the *Intelligenzaktion* and it targeted the intelligentsia during the first winter of the war. The names and addresses of political activists, professors, teachers, community leaders and other members of the nation's social élite had been collected by ethnic Germans before the war. They were listed in the Special Prosecution Book by the Gestapo's Central Unit IIP (Poland Office) and arrested soon after the invasion. Over 60,000 people were arrested by *Einsatzgruppen* and Self Protection paramilitary units and then taken to killing sites to be shot.

The Gestapo logged the rest of the intelligentsia either in a second Special Prosecution Book or on Investigation Detection Lists. A second nation-wide action started in May 1940, and the *Einsatzgruppen* rounded up another 30,000 people during 'Extraordinary Pacification Action' (*Außergewöhnliche Befriedung Aktion*), or AB Action, over the summer. Many were interrogated in prisons and held in new camps while others were taken to isolated locations and shot.

What follows are four types of action: an intimidation action, an intelligentsia action, an ethnic cleansing action and a politically motivated action.

An Intimidation Action in Kraków

SS-Obersturmbannführer Bruno Müller instructed Professor Tadeusz Lehr-Spławiński and the 180 professors of Kraków's Jagiellonian University to attend a lecture about German plans for Polish education on 6 November 1939. They were told they had broken the law by starting the new academic year without permission and were taken to the Montelupich prison. They were joined by the President of Kraków, Dr Stanisław Klimecki, before they were all transferred to Sachsenhausen concentration camp in Germany.

Protests resulted in the oldest men being released in February 1940, but the rest were sent to Dachau concentration camp. Most were set free by the beginning of 1941 but seventeen were already dead or would die from their privations shortly afterwards. The survivors later formed an underground university and one of their 800 students was Karol Wojtyła, the future Pope John Paul II.

An intelligentsia Action in Warsow

The Warsaw garrison surrendered on 28 September 1939 and Einsatzgruppe IV immediately arrested several hundred teachers and priests. Most were executed behind the parliament building on Wiejska Street over the winter. SS-Brigadeführer Lothar Beutel decided to carry out further executions at a secret location at the start of the Extraordinary Pacification Action in May 1940.

SS-Standartenführer Josef Meisinger's Gestapo officers made the arrests but then the prisoners were told they were being transferred by truck to another prison. They were handed their papers and belongings and given food for the journey so as not to alarm them. However, they found the Einsatzgruppe, Order Police and SS cavalry troopers waiting by pits in the Kampinos Forest, near Palmiry, twenty miles north-west of Warsaw. The authorities maintained the deception by informing families that their loved ones had died from natural causes.

Despite the secrecy, the news of the shootings soon got out because people living near the site saw or heard what was happening. Members of the Armed Struggle Union underground group even stole photographs of the murders from the executioners as evidence.

An Ethnic Cleansing Action in Saybusch County

Most people living in Żywiec County in Silesia in south-west Poland declared they were Polish during a census conducted at the end of 1939. So SS-Obersturmbannführer Fritz Arlt taxed them at a higher rate than the ethnic Germans.

Families were forced to hand over their money and valuables before they were escorted to the collection point (*Umschlagplatz*) in September 1940. They were assessed and classified into one of two groups: racially acceptable young men were sent to Germany to work while older men, women and children could stay. The rest were sent by train to Łódź where there was a second racial assessment, to see who could stay in the Wartheland Reich District. The undesirables were forwarded to the General Government, where they learnt that the Germans had branded them homeless criminals.

By December 1940, 19,000 Poles had been deported from Saybusch County, as it was now known, and their houses were cleaned by the few who had stayed behind. Around 3,200 ethnic Germans from Romania were moved in, but they spoke little German and had no interest in German culture. Similar projects across Poland were stopped when Hans Frank decided the General Government could not take any more refugees.

Another 30,000 Poles would be deported from Saybusch County over the next four years, and those deemed racially suitable were held in a Polish Camp (Polenlager) before they were sent to Germany to work; the rest were sent to work on Polish farms. Those who survived the war returned home to find that their houses had been wrecked and their livestock gone.

A Politically Motivated Action in the Soviet Union

The Red Army had captured tens of thousands of soldiers by the time the Polish military surrendered on 6 October 1939 (numbers range from 250,000 to 450,000). Many were released and a few escaped but around 125,000 were held in NKVD camps. The Wehrmacht and the Red Army then exchanged around 100,000 soldiers who came from their respective occupied zones.

Pre-war Poland had required university students to train as military reserve officers and that made them part of the intelligentsia. The NKVD's Prisoner Affairs Administration soon had 45,000 army officers, police officers, gendarmes, prison officers and scout leaders to interrogate. They were kept busy on forced labour for several months while they were repeatedly cross-examined about their political views.

On 5 March 1940 the head of the NKVD, Lavrentiy Beria, informed Stalin that 25,700 of the Polish officers had anti-Soviet views, and so six members of the Politburo signed their execution order. The head of the NKVD Prisoner of War Department, Major General Piotr Soprunenko, organised the transport, the executioners, and the digging of graves in the Katyń woods, twenty miles west of Smolensk. Day after day, lorry loads of shackled prisoners were taken into the woods and shot. The NKVD's chief executioner, Vasily Blokhin, would personally shoot 7,000 of them over twenty-eight days, making him the most prolific executioner in history. It is also believed that several thousand were murdered at other locations. By early May 1940, almost half the Polish officer corps were dead and their bodies hidden.

An agreement was signed by the Polish Prime Minister in exile, Władysław Sikorski, and the Soviet Ambassador to Britain, Ivan Mayski, shortly after Operation Barbarossa started in June 1941. It allowed for the release of thousands of Polish prisoners of war, which General Władysław Anders would organise into a 40,000 strong Polish army. The officers soon realised that many of their comrades were missing.

Józef Czapski was given the job of looking for them and he soon learnt about a mass grave at Katyń. He found the location but believed that only a few men were buried there. In April 1943, Rudolf von Gersdorff, a German officer at Army Group Centre's headquarters, heard about the mass graves, and his investigation uncovered the remains of several thousand Polish officers. Nazi Minister for Propaganda Joseph Goebbels had the news broadcast to the world to stir up problems between Poland and the Soviet Union; and it did.

Forensic experts investigated the mass graves, and while the Nazis continued to blame the Soviet Union, Moscow claimed the officers had been executed by the Germans in August 1941. The Polish Government-in-Exile called for an investigation by the International Red Cross, so Stalin cut diplomatic relations with Poland.

Army Group Centre withdrew from the Smolensk area in September 1943 and the NKVD moved in, intimidating witnesses and murdering the prisoners who had dug the graves. The Western Allies then agreed with the Extraordinary State Commission's announcement that the executions had been carried out by the Germans because they did not want to upset Moscow at a critical time in the war. They asked no further questions and even censored anyone who criticised the Soviet version of events.

Soviet lawyer General Roman Rudenko asked for the Katyń atrocity to be added to the list of German war crimes after the war but the American and British judges refused because of the ongoing debate over who was to blame. Instead a Red Army court-martial tried a small group of German soldiers in Leningrad and while one confessed to the crime, he later said he did so under duress.

A committee set up in the early 1950s concluded that the Soviets had carried out the Katyń massacre, but the subject was a forbidden topic in post-war communist Poland. The head of the KGB, Alexander Shelepin, destroyed evidence while the subject was entered in the Black Book of Censorship which listed what topics could not be discussed. The Polish trade union Solidarity erected the first memorial to Katyń in 1981, only to see it confiscated by the police. The Soviets rejected any responsibility for the executions, and they refused to accept it was a war crime until 1990. It was only in 2010 that Stalin and other Soviet officials were blamed for ordering the massacre.

A Slave Labour Force

Adults had to register with the Work Office and were allocated jobs. They had to work until they were 65 in the General Government and 70 if they lived in the annexed territories. Children had to register when they turned 14 in the General Government and at the age of 9 if they lived in the annexed territories.

Those who were arrested in one of the many round-ups were taken to one of the thirty work education camps (*Polenlager*), many of which were located in the industrial area of Silesia. They then experienced the forced labour regime with a six-week stint in what the Germans called a 'Labour Reformatory'. Work was physically hard and lasted twelve-hours a day, seven days a week. Roll calls were frequent, food was limited and punishments were harsh, and some succumbed to the mistreatment or malnutrition.

The survivors were then sent to the next factory which had requested more labourers. They continued to work long hours in dangerous conditions and were paid a fraction of what Germans received. Work groups were controlled by supervisors (either German helpers called *Hiwis* or privileged prisoners called *Kapos*) who meted out punishments in return for rewards.

The workers lived in basic barracks on a meagre diet of 700 kcal, consisting of watery soup, black bread and substitute (*ersatz*) coffee. Families were not allowed to send food or clothing to the camps and all mail was censored. There was little access to medical facilities when someone fell ill or were injured, and those unable to work were liable to be shot.

Many Poles were sent across the Reich to work and they had to carry their personal labour book with them, with a record of their work logged inside. They were allowed to leave the camp during their few free periods but a P badge (or Polish badge) on their clothes singled them out for abuse. They were forbidden to speak to Germans and sexual encounters carried harsh punishments. Polish men fraternising with German women would be shot while Polish women fraternising with German men would be made to work in a brothel.

Polish workers were often made to work in urban factories which were being targeted by the Allied air forces, while German workers were moved to safer rural locations. They sometimes endured round-the-clock bombing raids and often had to spend long periods repairing their places of work.

By 1945 hundreds of thousands of Poles of all ages (sources range from 1.5 million to 2.5 million) had been sent to the Reich for forced labour. Many more had worked across the General Government. They were all set free and gathered at a Displaced Persons camp for registration when the war ended, before heading back to Poland. Many returned to find their families dead, maimed or missing and their homes either destroyed or occupied. Many displaced persons were teenagers who had little education, just bodies broken by hard work. They never received any compensation for their hardships and had to start their lives from scratch. Many would suffer long term illnesses from their exertions across the Reich.

Concentration camps

The Germans established concentration camps across Poland during the early days of the occupation, such as Stutthof, Majdanek and Auschwitz. Tens of thousands of Poles were held in them for crimes against the state. Some were executed, some were put to work extending the camps or in nearby factories. However, many were deported to Germany and held in concentration camps there, such as Sachsenhausen, Gross-Rosen, Mauthausen, Neuengamme, Dachau, and Ravensbrück, until work was found for them.

SS-Obersturmbannführer Wilhelm Göcke ran a network of camps across Warsaw which could hold up to 40,000 prisoners at a time. They were used for slave labour and one of their jobs was to turn the Jewish ghetto area into a park following the uprising in April and May 1943. Many were worked to death or were shot; some think that an underpass on Bema Street could have been used as a gas chamber. SS-Hauptsturmführer Nikolaus Herbet became the commandant in September 1943 but the camp was closed down the following summer. It reopened briefly in January 1945 and would be used by the Polish Secret Police after the war.

SS-Obersturmführer Herbert Lange had organised the murder of infirmary patients in gas vans at Soldau in May and June 1940 and used the experience to set up Chełmno camp. The camp became a slave labour camp in the summer of 1941 and the workforce tested anti-tank guns and artillery as well as repaired tanks. Those unable to work were taken into the Białucki Forest and shot. Pregnant Polish women and orphans were held at the camp and the children were assessed to see if they could be adopted by a German family. The camp eventually closed in January 1945.

The prisoner of war camp was opened at Trawniki south-east of Lublin in July 1941; it was extended to accommodate 12,000 Polish Jews who would work in workshops the following year. Between September 1941 and July 1944 it housed around 5,000 men, many of them ex-Soviet soldiers from Belorussia and the Ukraine. They were coerced into carrying out the worst duties, including stopping ghetto uprisings, liquidating ghettos and working in the extermination camps. The fact that they spoke the language of those held in the ghettos and taken to the camps made them very useful.

An armaments factory was opened near Lwów in the autumn of 1941 and SS-Hauptsturmführer Fritz Gebauer established Janowska camp alongside. Jews were subjected to a selection process on arrival and those deemed unfit for work were sent to Piaski ravine to be shot or to Belzec to be gassed. The Sonderkommando rebelled when SS-Hauptsturmführer Friedrich Warzok shut the camp down in November 1943, but few escaped.

A camp was opened at Stutthof near Danzig at the end of 1941 to house members of the Polish intelligentsia; it was soon turned into a concentration camp. Over the months that followed, SS-Gruppenführer Fritz Katzmann opened dozens of sub-camps, where prisoners worked for the German Equipment Works and other businesses. Tens of thousands passed through the camp and it is believed that 85,000 people died there, many of them in mobile gas wagons or the gas chamber which was built in the camp in 1943.

SS-Obersturmführer Gottlieb Hering opened Poniatowa camp near Lublin in the autumn of 1942 to provide workers for the Walter Többens uniform factory. The camp became part of the Majdanek concentration camp in September 1943. The inmates were told to dig anti-tank trenches at the beginning of November 1943:it was a ruse to murder the camp population under Operation Harvest Festival, but the inmates soon realised what was happening. A rebellion in one of the barracks resulted in the shooting being spread over two days.

Adoption and Birthing Centres

The Nazis assessed children to see if they were racially acceptable to be raised as Germans. Those who passed the tests were taken from their families and sent to Germany, where families would raise them. The children of parents who had been executed were also assessed, but those considered unsuitable for adoption would be sent to an orphan camp or murdered. Very few survived. Those who lived with their German families often had no idea who their real parents were at the end of the war. Several years of indoctrination meant that they had little desire to return to Poland to find them.

Polish women were sent to work across Germany as forced labourers, starting in the spring of 1942. Those who had young children or babies had them placed in Foreign Children Nurseries (or Eastern Worker Children Nurseries) while they worked. Those who were already pregnant were not allowed to work in Germany, while those who fell pregnant while working had to abort their child.

Doctors checked the children and racially valuable children were given to German families. Those who were not deemed suitable were neglected and underfed while their mothers were at work; over half died. After spring 1943 all the children in the nurseries were considered to be parentless and their mothers lost what few rights they had. Soon afterwards, all Polish women who were unable to work after giving birth were murdered along with their babies.

A recruitment poster encouraging Polish ex-patriates to join the Blue Army.

ARMIA POLSKA WE FRANCYI
POLISH ARMY IN FRANCE
CENTRUM REKRUTACYJNE N̥ᵒ
RECRUITING CENTRE

Polish troops await the Red Army onslaught during the 'Miracle on the Vistula'.

General Józef Piłsudski inspects a guard of honour.

Józef Beck bows to Hitler during a meeting at his Alpine retreat, Berchtesgaden.

Rejewski, Różycki and Zygalski kept cracking the Enigma code for seven years before World War II.

Molotov signs the treaty of non–aggression while Ribbentrop and Stalin look over his shoulder.

The London newspapers report the invasion; two days later Britain declared war on Germany.

Stukas dive bomb Polish troops as they try to withdraw to new positions.

Hitler visits his generals to give praise and advice during the advance on Warsaw.

Terrified refugees try to escape the advancing columns of German tanks.

German and Polish police work side-by-side as they check identity cards.

Governor-General
Hans Frank ruled the
General Government
with an iron fist.

Security Service officers rush to grab a suspect before they can escape from their apartment.

Men are rounded up and put on lorries during an action, ready to be taken to a work site.

The Einsatzgruppen shoot members of the Polish intelligentsia at a secret location.

Men from an Einsatzgruppe search for partisans in the wilderness.

Polish pilots smile for the camera after successfully engaging German bombers.

Polish troops of Anders' Army raise their national flag over the ruins of Monte Cassino.

A foreign labourer's workbook and a patch and identity disc for a Polish worker.

The ghetto police keep order while men queue, hoping to be put onto a work detail.

Fences and barbed wire kept the Jews inside the ghetto until walls were built.

A patrol searches a cellar for Jews in hiding during a ghetto round-up.

Trains pulling cattle trucks deport the Jews to the extermination camps.

Home Army soldiers pose for the cameraman during the Warsaw Uprising.

Members of the Forest People parade at their camp in the wilderness.

Polish infantry en route to the front to serve with the Red Army.

Polish crews man Red Army tanks during the advance across Poland.

Partisans emerged to fight the Germans as the Red Army advanced, only to be arrested or executed.

Displaced Poles head home, unsure what to expect in their communist controlled country.

Tanks deployed on the streets during martial law.

General Jaruzelski announces martial law on 13 December 1981

Lech Wałęsa signals peace to the crowds at a gathering of Solidarity supporters.

Ghettos across the Greater Reich and the General Government after Operation Barbarossa.

Chapter 12

Burn out this Plague Dump

Creating and Controlling the Jewish Ghettos

Jewish Repression

The German priority during the first few months of the war was to murder the Polish intelligentsia. However, the military authorities made a special point of treating Jews more harshly than Christians if they happened to be caught in a round-up. There were plans afoot to remove the Jews from economic life, but areas had to be emptied of all non-Jews first, and then surrounded with a wall or fence to create ghettos.

Early regulations based on the Nuremburg Laws singled out the Jews and they all had to register with the authorities or face imprisonment or death. What follows are just a few of the many restrictions introduced while the ghettos were being prepared.

Jews were evicted from the best apartments, taking only what they could carry with them, while other owners had to register their property with the authorities. Their factories and businesses were either seized due to a breach of the law (sometimes falsely accused) or bought by German owners for a fraction of what they were worth. Professional Jews were disqualified from working with Germans or Poles, banned from working in factories or government institutions, only allowed to do manual jobs, and limited to a salary of 500 złoty a month. Families had to hand over valuables and foreign currency while their savings were seized. Germans and Poles were banned from buying from Jewish shops, further reducing their ability to earn money. Jews were also excluded from all trains, trams and buses, limiting their freedom and ability to work.

All adults and older children had to wear a Star of David armband or sew a yellow star onto their clothing after November 1939. It singled them out for attacks or arrests as they went about their daily business. They were the first to be taken to clear snow from the streets, clear up bomb damage and carry anything from requisitioned furniture supplies for the Germans.

The Germans implemented several things concerning the Jewish community as soon as they took control of a town or city. They set up a committee of community leaders, called the Jewish Council (*Judenrat*), to administer their orders and made all the Jews register with the authorities. They confiscated or burnt down synagogues, seized property, imposed fines and arrested men, either as hostages or for forced labour.

The Ghettos

Several months later, a ghetto was established, either in the Jewish quarter or in a rundown part of town, and the Jews were given a short time to move into the cramped accommodation. The Judenrat then had to enforce laws and regulations, submit reports, allocate living space, provide workers and raise revenue to pay fines. But they also tried to keep life going in the ghetto, by distributing food and running social institutions like hospitals, schools and orphanages. They would have to decide who to deport first when the time came.

Threats and difficult decisions sometimes led to council members being accused of favouritism and servility; sometimes justified and sometimes not. A few collaborated with the Nazis, hoping to save their friends and families, while others cooperated with the Jewish resistance groups. But they were all powerless to stop the deportations when the time came to liquidate their ghetto and they were murdered the same as the rest.

Most ghettos were surrounded by fences or walls and the gates were manned by the Order Police. The Germans offered better housing and rations to Jewish men who volunteered to help police with the ghettos. The Warsaw ghetto had 2,500 Jewish police who controlled 400,000 people while the Łódź ghetto had 1,200 to control 230,000. The auxiliaries wore an armband, a badge and sometimes a hat as symbols of their job, and they were armed with batons. They kept order during registration parades, helped to organise work details, and assisted during deportations. Some members tried to help the people while others abused their position to control the black market or accept bribes in exchange for favours. 'Group Thirteen' were a notorious group of ghetto police who searched for Jews who went outside the Warsaw ghetto.

The Housing Committee allocated living spaces, with several families crammed into apartments, creating unsanitary conditions. The Labour Committee then allocated work to those able to do so and their papers were marked accordingly. Many worked in nearby factories while others were employed around the ghetto. The SS, police and security services worked together to round up people to deport during actions. Non-workers were targeted first, and the sick, the infirm and children. They were either shot in the ghetto or taken to a collection point, escorted to the nearest train station, and loaded onto cattle wagons which took them to an extermination camp.

Jews from surrounding areas were often moved into the rooms left following an action. The constant round of selections, executions, deportations and new arrivals meant that no one felt safe. Over time the ghetto would reduce in size until the authorities decided it was time to close it and most of the remaining Jews would be deported to an extermination camp. A small group would be left behind to clear up the ghetto by removing the walls, repairing the buildings and decorating the apartments. They would often be shot before the Poles were moved into the defunct ghetto.

Pre-Barbarossa Ghettos

The Germans established ghettos in all the towns and cities across western and central Poland and here are brief accounts of what happened in the largest ones and other important ones. The first opened in October 1939, others opened as soon as areas had been prepared. Most opened in the spring of 1941, placing all the Jews behind walls before Operation Barbarossa was launched.

Piotrków Trybunalski Ghetto

The town was captured on 5 September 1939 and the ghetto opened five weeks later, the first of many across Poland. Oberbürgermeister Hans Drexler's first order to move in was ignored, so 28,000 Jews were forced into the few blocks over the weeks that followed. A curfew was used to limit movement until a fence had been erected and then SS-Hauptsturmführer Willy Blum had the sick and elderly shot to make way for Jews who would work in the nearby factories. Around 22,000 Jews were removed in October 1942 and while some were sent to work at Majdanek camp, near Lublin, most were gassed at Treblinka. Many of the remaining 3,500 workers would die over the months that followed.

Łódź Ghetto

The Wehrmacht entered Łódź on 8 September 1939 and four months later it was renamed Litzmannstadt, in memory of General Karl Litzmann, the general who had commanded an army in the area in 1914. Governor Friedrich Übelhör had started work on the ghetto in December 1939, although he made it clear he would have preferred to 'burn out this plague dump'. The police started random attacks on 8 February 1940 (known as 'Bloody Thursday') and around 350 Jews were murdered over the days that followed. Over 65,000 fled the city but the remaining 165,000 had been forced into the ghetto by the end of April. They were soon joined by another 40,000 who had been rounded up in the Warthegau district.

Chaim Rumkowski was head of the Council of Elders and he made sure that Hans Biebow's orders were carried out to the letter. King Chaim, as he became known, believed that hard work would make the Jews indispensable and he used the ghetto police to break up any strikes. There were frequent food shortages and 44,000 had died from starvation and disease by the time the ghetto's psychiatric patients were murdered in July 1941. At the end of the year, the Evacuation Committee was told to select 20,000 people who could not work and Rumkowski saw to it that the non-Łódź refugees left first.

The transports took the Jews to Chełmno, a new extermination camp which had opened thirty miles north of the city. Another 60,000 were deported over the summer, but suspicions were raised when their property started coming back to be sorted. There was consternation when Rumkowski announced that 13,000 children and 11,000 elderly had to be put on the next batch of trains and many families committed suicide rather than lose their loved ones. To make matters worse, the Jews saw over 12,000 children pass through adjacent orphans' camp, knowing what their fate would be.

A visit by Max Horn of the East Industry company in September 1943 sealed the fate of the remaining 90,000 Jews, because he thought the ghetto was badly managed and that the factories were turning out the wrong items. It meant that plans to relocate the workforce to another camp were dropped and the deportations to the extermination camps restarted.

Hans Bothmann reopened Chełmno as the Red Army drew closer and 25,000 Jews had been gassed by the time the rest were sent to Auschwitz-Birkenau. Rumkowski and his family were on the last transport, which left on 28 August 1944, and the Soviets only found a few hundred Jews alive when they arrived, who had hidden during the clearing up operations. Henryk Ross had taken many photographs of life inside the ghetto and he buried his negatives towards the end of the war. He returned to dig them up and they are an important archive of the 223,000 Jews who had once lived in Łódź.

Tomaszów Mazowiecki Ghetto

Kreishauptmann Lucas began moving the city's 15,000 Jews into the split site ghetto in May 1940 but it was December 1941 before the three areas were sealed. The transports took most to Treblinka, 150 miles to the north-east, in just two days in the spring of 1942. The remaining 1,000 workers were moved to Blizyn labour camp, south-west of Radom, when the ghetto closed in October 1942, but few survived the war.

Częstochowa Ghetto

The order to move 40,000 Jews into the Częstochowa ghetto, south of Łódź, was issued in April 1941 and its population grew to 48,000 over the next eighteen months. Most of the inmates were taken to Treblinka in two weeks in the autumn of 1942, while the sick and elderly were executed in the town. It left only 5,500 in the nearby factories and the Germans decided to relocate them in the summer of 1943. The Jewish Fighting Organisation rose upon 26 June and nearly 2,000 were killed, while 400 Jews were later executed in retaliation. About one third of 4,000 survivors were deported to concentration camps across Germany at the end of the year, but more prisoners arrived when the factories reopened in the autumn of 1944.

Three thousand prisoners were sent on the death march to Germany in January 1945 and none survived the harsh winter conditions. The camp guards abandoned the camp when the Red Army soldiers approached and they found over 5,000 starving prisoners in the ghetto.

Kielce Ghetto

The ghetto was opened in April 1941 and Jews from across south-west Poland had soon increased its population to 27,000. A planned uprising by the Jewish underground was betrayed by the chief of the Jewish police and so the liquidation went ahead in August 1942. Around 21,000 Jews were taken to Treblinka while those too sick to travel were shot in the ghetto. The remaining 2,000 workers were deported to Auschwitz or Buchenwald in September 1943.

Warsaw Ghetto

Around 270,000 Jews were living in the centre of Warsaw when the Germans invaded Poland on 1 September 1939. Over 30,000 people died and many more were injured during the Luftwaffe bombings over the days that followed. Another 90,000 refugees entered Warsaw as the Wehrmacht closed in, but the military garrison surrendered on 29 September.

SS-Standartenführer Josef Meisinger was appointed the SS and Police Leader of the city in November and became known as the 'Butcher of Warsaw'. His men moved 113,000 Poles out of the central Muranów district to make way for the largest ghetto in Poland. Einsatzgruppe IV then began moving Warsaw's 138,000 Jews into the ghetto.

Work started on the walls in April 1940 and gates on Chłodna Street connected the two parts until they were replaced by a footbridge. Over 400,000 people had been squeezed into an area measuring 1.3 square miles by the time they were complete at the end of the year. It meant an average of seven people were living in each room. Many Jews were then put to work in factories across the city and war profiteers like Walter Többens employed up to 15,000 Jews.

Food supplies to the ghetto were stopped in January 1941, so it was down to smugglers to buy it from black-marketeers operating outside. The security services were always on the lookout for Jews hunting for food while 3,000 ghetto police kept order inside. Many died of starvation and disease but the community leaders did their best to organise hospitals, soup kitchens, orphanages and refugee centres. They also set up synagogues, schools, libraries and recreation facilities.

On 22 July 1942, SS and Police Chief Ferdinand von Sammern-Frankenegg deployed SS and police units ready to carry out Great Action Warsaw (*Gross Aktion Warsaw*). Resettlement Commissioner Sturmbannführer Hermann Höfle told the Judenrat leader Adam Czerniaków that transports would start leaving the following day, the Jewish holiday of Tisha B'Av. Czerniaków could not face choosing who would have to go and he committed suicide, so Marc Lichtenbaum had to decide.

Around 5,000 people were escorted to the collection point, where two trains took them to Treblinka camp, fifty miles north-east. The largest number were seized after queuing for a false promise of food, while the last batch, which included the Jewish police and their families, left on the feast of Yom Kippur. Around 260,000 had been taken to Treblinka in nine weeks.

Mińsk Mazowiecki Ghetto

Around 7,000 Jews were moved into the ghetto from the area east of Warsaw in October 1940. Most were transported to Treblinka in August

1942, while the ill and infirm were shot in the town. A few hundred men were left behind to clear up the ghetto but they too were shot when the work ended in June 1943. Partisans got their revenge by assassinating the town's Gestapo chief, SS-UnterstURMführer Schmidt, a month later.

Radom Ghetto

SS-Gruppenführer Fritz Katzmann was appointed SS and Police Chief in November 1939 and he started by executing the Jewish leaders and fining their community a huge amount. Many of Kraków's Jews were moved into the city and over 33,000 were forced into the two ghetto areas in the spring of 1941. The smaller Glinice ghetto was liquidated by August 1942 and then it was the turn of the larger one. Most of Jews were transported to Treblinka while the small number kept behind to clean up the ghetto had either been murdered or deported by June 1944.

Opole Lubelskie Ghetto

Around 10,000 Jews were moved into the ghetto in March 1941 but many died in the typhus epidemic which swept through the overcrowded area. There were deportations in the spring of 1942 but most were taken to Sobibór in October 1942.

Kraków Ghetto

The treatment of Kraków's Jews has been well documented in the 1982 book *Schindler's Ark* and the 1993 film *Schindler's List*, but here are the salient points. The city's SS and Police Leader, Julian Scherner, made all the city's 68,000 Jews register with the authorities. Laws were then introduced to limit their ability to work and earn money. Hans Frank made Kraków his headquarters and he announced it would be the 'racially cleanest' city in the General Government in May 1940. Around 23,000 Jews were allowed to leave the city in the summer, to join family or friends living in rural areas, but another 43,000 were forced to leave before the end of the year. Only 15,000 essential workers and their families were permitted to stay in Kraków and they were forced to move into Podgórze ghetto in March 1941. A labour office was set up for those who worked outside the ghetto, including those employed at the nearby German Enamel Works owned by the war profiteer Oskar Schindler.

The Jews from the villages around Kraków were moved back into the city at the beginning of 1942, overcrowding the ghetto even more. On 1 June 1942, SS-Obersturmbannführer Willi Haase deployed police and SS around the ghetto and they rounded up 7,000 Jews who were taken to Bełżec extermination camp.

SS-Untersturmführer Amon Göth liquidated the Kraków ghetto in March 1943: 2,000 sick and infirm were murdered while 8,000 were moved to Płaszów camp. Oskar Schindler paid bribes to keep his workforce at his German Enamel Works, where they avoided most of the excesses of the SS guards.

Płaszów was closed in the summer of 1944 and the remaining Jews were taken to concentration camps across the Reich. The camp was demolished while all the corpses were dug up and burnt. There was nothing to be found when the Red Army reached Kraków in January 1945. Schindler meanwhile had again paid bribes so he could relocate his 1,200-strong workforce to his home town of Brünnlitz in the Sudetenland, where most survived the war.

Tarnów Ghetto

The Wehrmacht entered Tarnów, east of Kraków, on 8 September 1939. The Judenrat was formed in November 1940 and its first task was to raise money to pay the large fine placed on their community. The ghetto opened in March 1941 and there were soon 40,000 Jews crammed inside. Around 13,500 were transported to Bełżec in June 1942 while another 10,000 who were too sick to make the journey were shot in the town.

Another 8,000 were taken to Bełżec in September 1942, but the people were getting suspicious: some joined the Young Guard underground, others escaped into the woods to join the partisans. The ghetto was closed in September 1943 and 3,000 were sent work in Plaszów camp near Kraków while another 7,000 were sent to Auschwitz-Birkenau to be murdered.

Będzin and Sosnowiec Ghettos

The 30,000 Jews of Będzin and Sosnowiec were joined in two ghettos by another 15,000 from across Silesia in July 1940. The Sosnowiec ghetto was moved next to the Będzin ghetto over the winter of 1942-3 so they could work in new military factories. The Jews hoped they would survive if they worked hard, but 40,000 were deported to Auschwitz-Birkenau in the summer 1943. An uprising by the Jewish Combat Organization at the beginning of August resulted in around 400 fighters being killed; it only delayed the departure of the final trains.

Lublin Ghetto

SS and Police Chief Odilo Globočnik started evicting the Jews from the suburbs around his headquarters in 1940, forcing them to live with friends or family in rural areas. He believed they should 'feed themselves and be supported by their countrymen, as they have enough food. They should be allowed to starve, if this does not work.'

He moved 34,000 into the ghetto the following spring to make way for the soldiers moving into the city ahead of Operation Barbarossa. The community members were held as hostages in Lublin Castle to ensure the Jews' cooperation during their stay. Most of the Jews were deported to Bełżec, eighty miles to the south-east, in the spring of 1942. Another 4,000 were put to work sorting possessions in Majdanek concentration camp, outside the city.

The ghetto was due to be closed in the autumn of 1943, but the uprising in the Warsaw ghetto and at the Sobibór and Treblinka camps meant that underhanded methods were used to murder the Jews. Sturmbannführer Christian Wirth made the inmates dig anti-tank trenches outside the city when they were in fact digging graves. Around 43,000 people were shot on 3 November 1943, during the largest single day massacre committed by German troops: Operation Harvest Festival (*Aktion Erntefest*).

Post Barbarossa Ghettos

Tens of thousands of Jews had fled into the Soviet zone to escape the German invasion in September 1939. Many welcomed the arrival of the Red Army and some even helped round up the Polish intelligentsia when the NKVD arrived. The Poles were the NKVD's main target until Operation Barbarossa was launched on 22 June 1941. The Jews were then attacked by *Einsatzgruppen* and Order Police who were following the Wehrmacht. Ghettos would be organised over the months that followed and then the Jews were taken away on transports. They were either taken to one of the extermination camps to be gassed or into the woods to be shot.

Wilno Ghetto

The Wehrmacht reached Wilno (Vilna and now Vilnius) on 26 June 1941, finding over 60,000 Jews in the city. The Einsatzgruppe and their Lithuanian helpers (called *hapunes* or snatchers) went on the rampage, murdering around 20,000 Jews over the next five weeks.

Oberscharführer Horst Schweinberger then staged a shooting, called the 'Great Provocation', on 31 August 1941, to give an excuse to clear the ghetto area. Thousands of people were dragged from their homes and killed on the streets, others were shot at Ponary on the outskirts of the city. Many more were killed when the remaining 20,000 were forced into the two ghetto areas a week later.

The United Partisan Organisation was formed in January 1942 and they stuck by their motto, 'we will not go like sheep to the slaughter', as they tried to fight back. But they failed to stop the murder of the Jews who were too sick or old to work at Ponary in October 1942, many on the feast day of Yom Kippur. More Jews were moved in from the surrounding area, but new actions resulted in another 20,000 Jews being shot early in 1943, many of them by the Lithuanian Special Squads (*Ypatingasis Būrys*). The partisans escaped into the woods when Oberscharführer Bruno Kittel sent the remaining 7,000 Jews to other camps in the summer of 1943.

Białystok Ghetto

The city was captured by the Wehrmacht in June 1941 and the executions began straight away. The Jewish community was accused of assisting the Red Army and over 3,000 were shot by an Einsatzgruppe when the remaining 43,000 were herded inside the ghetto a month later. The Anti-Fascist Military Organisation formed inside the ghetto in 1942 in Białystok and it helped a few people escape.

In February 1943 over 7,500 Jews were sent to Majdanek to work, 10,000 were transported to Treblinka to be gassed and 2,000 sick and elderly were shot. Around 1,000 children were also sent via Theresienstadt to Auschwitz-Birkenau. The deportations continued until the Anti-Fascist Military Organisation attacked on 16 August 1943 and they continued to fight until the ghetto was liquidated a month later. Only a few of the resistance fighters escaped to join partisan groups.

Nowogródek Action

The Wehrmacht entered Nowogródek on 30 June 1941 and an Einsatzgruppe arrived in December. They shot around 9,500 Jews and deported another 500 for slave labour.

Łachwa Ghetto

The Wehrmacht entered the town, south of Minsk, on 8 July 1941 and had moved 2,500 Jews into a ghetto by April 1942. A resistance group was formed by the inmates when they heard about the massacres and they prepared to fight. The final straw came when they were told that pits were being dug on the outskirts of the town. The Germans told the Judenrat they would be spared if they cooperated but Dov Lopatyn replied, 'either we all live, or we all die,' and warned his community. The German soldiers were attacked when they entered on 2 September 1942 and while 650 Jews were killed in the first Jewish uprising of the war, only 500 were taken to the execution site because around 1,000 had escaped into the Pripet (or Pinsk) marshes. Many were tracked down, others starved to death, and only a few dozen survived the war.

Brest-Litovsk Ghetto

SS-Obergruppenführer Karl Schöngarth's Einsatzgruppe executed 5,000 citizens in three days, and the Order Police shot many more as they passed through the city. A ghetto for 18,000 Jews was opened in December 1941 but the Germans demanded a huge amount of money to keep it open in the autumn of 1942. The Jews paid the ransom but they were still transported into the Bronna Góra forest, 75 miles north-east of the city, and executed.

Pińsk Ghetto

The Wehrmacht entered Pińsk on 4 July and the Waffen SS responded to partisan actions in the area by executing 11,000 Jewish men in three days in August. The remaining 20,000 Jews were locked inside the ghetto in April 1942 but the 3,500 sick and infirm were taken into the woods and shot a few weeks later. Jews from the surrounding settlements were then moved in to take their place.

The Jewish resistance were so active that local auxiliary police had to be deployed to help the Order Police keep order in the ghetto. The authorities had had enough by October 1942 and trains took three days to transport 17,000 Jews into the Bronna Góra woods to be shot. A Sonderkommando had to exhume and cremate the bodies in March 1944, before they too were shot.

Kowel Ghetto

Kowel was captured at the end of June 1941 and the killings began immediately. The Jews were fined a huge amount before they were moved into two ghettos, one for the workers and the other for those without work permits, in May 1942. The non-workers were shot in a nearby quarry a few days later. Another fine was levied and all valuables had to be handed over before the executions began in earnest; 8,000 Jews were executed in the forest near Bakhiv on 19 August alone. Everyone from the Kowel ghetto had been murdered by the end of September.

Łuck Ghetto

The NKVD executed 4,000 prisoners when Operation Barbarossa began on 22 June 1941 and then left the town. The *Einsatzgruppen* and the Ukrainian People's Militia then moved in and blamed the Jews for the atrocities and shot 2,000 of them. Around 20,000 Jews had been forced into the ghetto by the end of the year but most of them were taken into the Górka Połonka forest and shot in August 1942. The remaining 3,000 carried on working to the end of the year and those destined to leave on the last transport died fighting back.

Lwów Ghetto

The city's Jewish community of 330,000 had been swelled by 150,000 refugees from the German-occupied part of the Poland. The Soviets murdered 7,000 civilians before they withdrew from Lwów ahead of Operation Barbarossa in June 1941 and then the Germans incited the Ukrainians to attack the Jews. Around 4,000 had been murdered before the *Einsatzgruppen* joined in and they executed another 8,500 over the weeks that followed.

SS-Gruppenführer Fritz Katzmann opened the ghetto in November 1941 and the security forces killed many as they escorted them to the area.

The transports started taking the Jews to Bełżec in March 1942 and the last one left in June 1943.

Reporting the Holocaust

Second Lieutenant Jan Kozielewski disguised that fact that he was an officer when he was taken prisoner by the Red Army in September 1939. He was then handed over to the Germans because he had been born in Łódź but escaped from their camp in November. Kozielewski headed to Warsaw to join the underground movement, Poland's Victory Service, and used the name Jan Karski. He travelled to Paris several times with reports on the conditions inside occupied Poland. He was even smuggled into the Warsaw ghetto on two occasions in 1942, to see what was happening to the Jews, and then escaped with his findings.

Prisoners Eugeniusz Bendera, Kazimierz Piechowski, Stanisław Gustaw Jaster and Józef Lempart stole SS uniforms and drove a staff car out of Auschwitz on 20 June 1942. They were carrying a report on conditions inside the camp written up by Witold Pilecki who had been smuggled into the camp.

Karski's and Pilecki's information was written up as 'The Mass Extermination of Jews in German occupied Poland' by Foreign Minister Edward Raczynski. It was delivered to the governments of the United Nations in December 1942 and to several other government and civic leaders. Karski met many western politicians, including President Franklin D. Roosevelt, but few believed the report because it seemed so far-fetched at the time.

The Warsaw Ghetto Uprising

We have seen how the Jewish resistance organisations sometimes fought to stop the deportations from the ghettos. Their attempts were all but futile because they lacked the weapons to do more than kill a few guards and delay the journey to the extermination camps. However, the uprising in the Warsaw ghetto in the spring of 1943 was the notable exception.

The Warsaw ghetto held around 400,000 people and it was under the control of the SS and Police Chief SS-Gruppenführer Odilo Globocnik, and head of the SD and SiPo SS-Standartenführer Ludwig Hahn. Adam Czerniaków had committed suicide in July 1942 after hearing that the transports were about to begin. Around 300,000 had been taken to Treblinka by September, when news that they were being murdered reached the ghetto. So 400 members of the Jewish Military Union collected their machine guns, rifles and grenades, while 200 members of the Jewish Combat Organisation armed themselves with pistols and petrol bombs. They then joined the Home Army and were given weapons and training.

The Germans restarted the deportations in January 1943, but a revolt reduced the number of deportees. The resistance fighters built bunkers and executed collaborators until the police and SS auxiliaries entered the ghetto on 19 April 1943, the eve of Passover. This time they came under fire and sixty were hit while two armoured vehicles were disabled. SS-Brigadeführer Jürgen Stroop replaced SS-Oberführer Ferdinand von Sammern-Frankenegg and he assembled hundreds of soldiers, paramilitaries and members of the emergency services, who were supported by tanks and artillery. He was determined to remove the Polish and Jewish Military Union flags flying over the ghetto and then kill everyone inside its walls.

Tanks and armoured cars supported the infantry as they moved from block to block, but the Jews time and again escaped along tunnels and sewers to their next position. The Home Army and the People's Guard assisted by smuggling arms and ammunition to the Jews, while attacking German units outside the walls.

Resistance had started to crumble by the end of April and the Jewish Military Union escaped through tunnels, hoping to fight again. One by one the groups were surrounded, as the Germans used dogs, explosives, smoke bombs, flame throwers and water to flush them out of their hideouts. They found the Jewish Combat Organisation command post on 8 May; its members had all committed suicide.

The uprising ended on 16 May 1943 when Stroop pressed the detonator to blow up Warsaw's Great Synagogue. Around 19,000 Jews had perished in the fighting and another 50,000 were taken away on transports. Many were gassed in Treblinka but a few brave souls joined the mass escape from the camp on 2 August 1943; few survived the war.

The month-long uprising was the largest Jewish act of resistance in World War II. The ghetto buildings were demolished soon afterwards and a concentration camp was opened on the site. Sammern-Frankenegg was assassinated by Yugoslav partisans in September 1943. Warsaw's Governor, Ludwig Fischer, was executed in 1947, and Stroop met the same fate in 1952.

The location of the Operation Reinhard camps and other major extermination camps.

Chapter 13

Operation Reinhard

Organising the Jewish Holocaust

The Final Solution to the Jewish Question

Senior representatives of the Nazi government departments and SS leaders attended a meeting in the Berlin suburb of Wannsee on 20 January 1942. The meeting was called by the director of the Reich Main Security Office, SS-Obergruppenführer Reinhard Heydrich, and organised by SS-Obersturmbannführer Adolph Eichmann, the head of Sub-Department IV-B4, the office for Jewish affairs.

Eichmann explained that there were 5.5 million Jews living in the Third Reich and annexed areas while there were a similar number in areas which they planned to invade. Heydrich explained how his commanding officer, Reichsführer Heinrich Himmler, had stopped emigration from German-held territories, so they had to find a new way to get rid of the Jews. He explained the actions which had so far been carried out by the *Einsatzgruppen*, as well as the difficulties arising from the shooting of tens of thousands of men, women and children.

Heydrich made it clear that the SS were now running the operation and that he expected cooperation from all the departments. Jews would be evacuated (the code word for deportation) to transit camps across the General Government area, where they would be assessed. Then there was a lengthy discussion about defining Jews and a mixed-race people (known as *Mischlings*). Heydrich said that draconian measures would be implemented based on a person's blood relations, their physical appearance and their religious views.

The Jews would be sent to new camps for special treatment (the code word for murder), which would be carried out using a secret method which had been used across Germany, Austria and Poland for some time: gassing. Around 300,000 incurable hospital patients had been subjected to involuntary euthanasia using carbon monoxide under the T4 Programme between September 1939 and August 1941. Testing with gas vans was already underway at the Chełmno camp but there were plans to streamline the murder process, to speed up the annihilation of Europe's Jewry. After an hour of information, Heydrich and Eichmann answered questions for half an hour. The secret meeting led to the drafting of the 'Final Solution to the Jewish Question'.

Himmler told Otto Globočnik, SS and Police Leader of Lublin, to start building an extermination camp at Bełżec, 100 miles south-east of the city, in October 1941. SS-Sturmbannführer Christian Wirth, a veteran of the T-4 euthanasia programme, had completed the project by the following March. Similar work began at Treblinka, Sobibór and Majdanek soon afterwards in preparation for the mass murder of Europe's Jews. Wirth lived up to his nickname of 'Christian the Terrible' and would be promoted to inspector of all the camps in August 1942. Globočnik was promoted to run the whole extermination programme. It was codenamed Operation Reinhard because Heydrich had died following an assassination attempt by Czech and Slovak agents in May 1942.

SS-Sturmbannführer Ernst Lerch ran Globočnik's office and he kept Berlin informed about progress. SS-Hauptsturmführer Hermann Höfle trained the camp staff, instructing them to keep their work secret, while experienced T4 staff supervised the gassing. Each camp had around one hundred auxiliaries, called *Hiwis* (an abbreviation of the German word for willing helpers, *Hilfswillige*), to organise the foulest jobs. SS-Hauptsturmführer Karl Streibel had recruited a mixture of ethnic Germans from Lithuania, Latvia and the Ukraine as well as several Red Army prisoners of war. They spoke a mixture of Polish, Russian and Ukrainian, and could order the Jews around in their own language. Over 5,000 were trained at Trawniki training camp, south-east of Lublin, and detachments served at all the extermination camps.

Sobibór opened in May 1942, followed by Treblinka two months later, and the staff organised some prisoners into Special Commands (*Sonderkommando*) to carry out the worst tasks. Some helped the Jews off the trains, some made them undress, others shaved their hair while more searched their luggage for valuables. The worst job was to remove the bodies from the gas chambers. Some removed gold teeth from the corpses, others organised the burial process. The Sonderkommando were executed at regular intervals to maintain the camp's secrets.

Skilled workers were selected from the first trains to reach Lublin because there was a shortage of labour in the General Government. Globočnik's deputy, Hermann Höfle, supported the policy but nobody wanted to feed the workers, so everyone on the future transports went straight to one of the extermination camps. Operation Reinhard ended in November 1943 with the deaths by gassing of over two million Jews, most of them from Poland. The approximate number of deaths were:

Bełżec, 600,000   Sobibór, 250,000
Treblinka, 850,000   Lublin/Majdanek, 130,000 (78,000 confirmed)

The camp staff and guards were then sent to northern Italy to put down partisan activity. Some were tried and sentenced at the Nuremberg trials but most escaped trial and returned to normal lives after the war.

In January 1943 the British Code and Cipher Centre at Bletchley Park deciphered a telegram from Höfle to Eichmann. It listed the 1,274,166 arrivals at the Reinhard camps by the end of 1942, using only letters for the four camp names. The message was logged but its significance was not realised until many years after the war.

Organisation of the Camps

The Reinhard camps were based on a pilot project at Chełmno (Kulmhof) which had been in operation for several months. The three camps at Bełżec, Sobibór, and Treblinka simplified the murder process by having a train deliver the Jews to an isolated camp hidden in woods. Twenty wagons at a time, each containing one hundred people, were shunted along a siding to a platform which was made to look like a working station. But the whole area was surrounded by watchtowers, barbed-wire fences and minefields, so no one could escape.

Around twenty-five German SS and police officials ran the camp while one hundred auxiliaries supervised the Sonderkommando as they helped the passengers off the train. To begin with, the men were separated from the women and children in the reception area, but this was stopped when the victims suspected what was about to happen. A few with appropriate skills would be selected to work in the camp but the elderly and sick were loaded onto wagons and taken to a bogus infirmary where they were shot. The rest had to hand over their valuables and luggage before they were made to undress and have their heads shaved.

The Jews then followed a short path or corridor to a building which had been disguised as a shower block. But pipes from Red Army tank engines soon filled the rooms with carbon monoxide, asphyxiating those crammed inside in less than thirty minutes. The Sonderkommando then had to remove the corpses and take gold teeth from their mouths and valuables from other orifices. A mini railway carried the bodies from the gas chamber to the grave site. Bełżec and Treblinka used excavators to dig the huge pits.

The rest of the Sonderkommando sorted the belongings taken from the victims' cases and repaired what they could so it could be recycled. SS-Obergruppenführer August Frank issued a memorandum on 26 September 1942 detailing where the Jews' possessions and valuables were to be sent. Cash, precious metals and jewels were to be delivered to the Main Economic and Administration Office. The gold and valuable items ended up in the Reichsbank's secret Melmer account (named after Bruno Melmer), the Gold Pool or Nazi Germany's monetary reserve.

Valuable items and furs were to be repaired and cleaned before they were forwarded to the same office, silks were to be sent to the Reich Ministry of Economics, spectacles and artificial limbs were to go to the Reich Medical Services. All clothing had to be repaired, checked for hidden valuables and the yellow stars removed before they were sent to the Ethnic German Coordination Centre so they could be given to settlers. The same applied to bedding and other household items, although some cloth items were sent to military units.

Altogether Operation Reinhard earned the SS Main Economic and Administrative Office around 180 million German Reichsmarks' worth of property (now in the region of £2billion) in less than two years. However, there was widespread corruption at the camps and two commandants were arrested and executed for defrauding the state. The fact that they had overseen the murder of tens of thousands of people was ignored.

Chełmno Camp

The camp was opened in December 1941, some thirty miles north-west of Łódź. It would not be part of Operation Reinhard, but it was the pilot project for the extermination camps. SS-Obergruppenführer Wilhelm Koppe gave the order to build the camp and while SS-Standartenführer Ernst Damzog organised the round-ups across the Poznań district, SS-Hauptsturmführer Herbert Lange ran the camp.

The Jews from the Łódź ghetto were taken to Kolo railway station and then transferred to a narrow-gauge train which took them to Powiercie. Trucks then drove them to a nearby manor house where they were told they were going to have a shower while their clothes were disinfected.

After stripping, they walked along a corridor and, unknown to them, up a ramp into the back of a truck. The driver then headed two miles into the forest while the carbon monoxide from the engine gassed those inside, and then a Sonderkommando put the corpses into the grave pits; the Sonderkommando were regularly murdered to keep the operation a secret.

SS-Hauptsturmführer Hans Bothmann took over the camp in April 1942. The summer heat made the smell at the forest site unbearable, so the decision was taken to cremate the bodies. The Sonderkommando was increased in size so the grave pits could be opened and the bodies burnt. Chełmno closed in March 1943 and both the manor house and the crematorium ovens in the forest were demolished. The labourers were then shot; the last of over 150,000 people killed at the camp.

Belżec Camp

Work started on the first Reinhard camp in November 1941. The camp had been sited between Zamość and Lwów in south-east Poland because it had rail connections to Lublin, Krakow and Lwów. SS-Sturmbannführer Christian Wirth was ready for the first transports in March 1942 and many more came from south and south-east Poland over the weeks that followed.

Around 150,000 Jews had been gassed by the time Wirth had been promoted to inspect all the Reinhard camps in June 1942. He was replaced by SS-Obersturmführer Gottlieb Hering, who oversaw the deaths of another 300,000 Jews, including many from across Europe, over the next six months.

The discovery of the remains of 20,000 Polish officers at Katyń in April 1943 meant the Nazis had to rethink how to hide the evidence of Operation Reinhard. Special Action 1005 (*Sonderaktion 1005*) involved the digging up of tens of thousands of decomposing corpses by Corpse Commandos (*Leichen Kommando*s). The remains were cremated on funeral pyres, the bone fragments were ground up in machines, and the ashes were scattered. The buildings had been removed by June and all the inmates were either shot on site or gassed at Sobibór.

Treblinka Camp

Treblinka I labour camp had opened next to a main railway line fifty miles north-east of Warsaw in November 1941. SS-Untersturmführer Dr Irmfried Eberl (another member of the T4 euthanasia programme) opened an extermination camp in the nearby woods in July 1942. Trains stopped at Malkinia station and then twenty wagons at a time were shunted into the fake station. However, the trains arrived too fast, creating chaos across the camp and SS-Hauptsturmführer Franz Stangl (from Sobibór) had to take over.

Over 600,000 Jews from the Warsaw and Radom ghettos had been gassed when the decision to exhume and burn the bodies was made in the autumn of 1942. Another 300,000 Jews from Bialystok, Lublin and across the rest of Europe had been gassed by the time the operations ended in the summer of 1943. The Sonderkommando realised they were going to be killed, so they staged a breakout on 2 August and while over 300 escaped, many were rounded up and killed.

SS-Untersturmführer Kurt Franz was sent to Treblinka to close the camp. The new Sonderkommando were all shot when the work was completed in November 1943. The labour camp continued to operate until the Red Army approached in July 1944.

Sobibór Camp

The camp was built next to the railway line connecting Włodawa and Chełm in south-east Poland. SS-Obersturmführer Franz Stangl opened the camp in May 1942. He was nicknamed the 'White Death' because he often wore a white uniform. He had overseen the gassing of tens of thousands of Jews from the Lublin area before he was transferred to Treblinka.

SS-Hauptsturmführer Franz Reichleitner took over and his first task was to have all the bodies dug up and cremated. Altogether around 225,000 Jews from across Europe had been murdered by the time the Sonderkommando heard that Bełżec's workforce had been murdered when the camp closed. So they murdered several guards and around 300 escaped on 14 October 1943; most were captured and murdered. The camp was then torn down and the rest of the workforce were shot.

Majdanek Camp

SS-Standartenführer Karl-Otto Koch opened Majdanek camp on the outskirts of Lublin in October 1941. It became the sorting and storage depot for the possessions and valuables taken from the tens of thousands of Jews murdered at the three Reinhard camps. A gas chamber designed to murder with the fumigation chemical Zyklon B was opened in March 1942, but Koch was arrested for corruption and murder the following August.

SS-Sturmbannführer Max Koegel ran the camp until November while his replacement, SS-Obersturmführer Hermann Florstedt, was also arrested for corruption and murder. His final act had been to organise the shooting of nearly 18,500 camp inmates on 3 and 4 November 1943 as part of Operation Harvest Festival. SS-Obersturmbannführer Martin Weiss then spent the next six months closing the main camp and its satellites. Altogether over 100,000 people had died (78,000 confirmed) in Majdanek by the time SS-Obersturmbannführer Arthur Liebehenschel was ordered to demolish the camp. He failed, and the Red Army captured it intact in July 1944.

Ending Operation Reinhard

News of the gas chambers reached the Jews left in the Lublin ghetto by the autumn of 1943. There had been a revolt at Treblinka in August and a breakout at Sobibór in October, and the SS were worried there could be more as the Red Army moved closer. So SS-Sturmbannführer Christian Wirth ordered the murder of the remaining Jews working around Lublin, including those working at the Trawniki, Majdanek and Poniatowa camps. SS and Police Leader of Lublin, SS-Gruppenführer Jakob Sporrenberg, made them dig anti-tank trenches on 3 November, not realising they were digging their graves. Majdanek and Trawniki were cleared in a single day but some of the Poniatowa barracks had to be burnt down with the prisoners still inside the following day. Around 42,000 Polish Jews were killed in this, the largest operation of its kind carried out by German soldiers. Operation Harvest Festival brought Operation Reinhard to an end after eighteen deadly months.

Globočnik and Lerch would also be given responsibility for General Plan East, the deportation of Poles to the General Government to make way for German settlers. However, the Operation Reinhard team ended the war in Italy, where they rounded up and murdered political opponents, Jews and partisans. Wirth was assassinated by Yugoslav partisans in May 1944; Globočnik committed suicide at the end of the war. Hermann Höfle did the same when he was eventually arrested in 1962 but Lerch repeatedly escaped justice due to a lack of witnesses; he died in 1997.

Auschwitz-Birkenau Camp

The most infamous extermination camp of them all was not part of Operation Reinhard. Instead it started as a prison camp for Polish intelligentsia and then for Soviet soldiers. It became a collection hub for Jews from across Europe as Reinhard was being closed down and they would be divided into those who would be worked to death and those who would be gassed. The Auschwitz-Birkenau complex would eventually become the location where the most people were murdered in history.

Oswiecim stands close to the confluence of the Rivers Sola and Vistula, where there were many rich resources that the Third Reich wanted to exploit. Rudolf Höss was appointed commandant of a concentration camp based in the local army barracks at the beginning of May 1940. The first Polish prisoners arrived six weeks later and they were put to work building their own prison. Before long the camp had fences, watchtowers, a post office, a kitchen, a laundry, a hospital and administration buildings. But it also had an operating theatre for experiments, a punishment block, an execution wall, gallows and crematorium. A small gas chamber was soon added.

Criminals ran the work gangs, and there were many injuries and deaths as the men carried out hard physical labour at break-neck speed. Once the fences were electrified, it was time to put the inmates to work in the local sand and gravel pits, in factories and on farms. Meanwhile Auschwitz was being Germanized by deporting the Jews and building new houses for immigrants who would work in the surrounding factories. Eventually 6,500 Germans would live in the town and few knew anything about what was happening in the nearby camp.

Himmler visited Auschwitz in March 1941 and there was talk of expanding the town and the camp. There may have also been talk of a second camp for 100,000 prisoners at nearby Brzezinka but the plans were not formally discussed until the autumn. It would be built by thousands of Red Army officers and political commissars captured during Operation Barbarossa and would be called Birkenau. The new camp had 174 barrack blocks, kitchens, toilets, washrooms and delousing buildings. Altogether it would be able to house 130,000 prisoners crammed into tiny bunks, if it was ever completed. The work was back-breaking and only a few hundred of the Soviet prisoners would survive the winter of 1941-2 as they dug ditches, demolished farms and built barracks. The first German prisoners arrived in March 1942 and more barracks were added to accommodate them, all surrounded by electrified fences and guard towers. Internal fences kept the men and women apart, while quarantine areas were used to stop the spread of typhus.

Following the Wannsee Conference on 20 January 1942, plans were put in place to turn Birkenau into an extermination centre capable of murdering the tens of thousands of Jews currently held in ghettos across Europe.

The first gassings were carried out in two small houses, called the Red House and the White House, outside the wire. The Jews were told to strip ready to be disinfected in shower rooms, only they would be gassed with Zyklon B.

The mass graves had become a serious health problem by the time Himmler made his second visit in July 1942, so Sonderkommando were put to work exhuming and burning the corpses in incineration pits. There was talk of increasing the capacity of Birkenau in the autumn of 1942, so work was started on purpose-built buildings which had undressing rooms, gas chambers and crematoria.

The Reinhard camps were being closed down by the autumn of 1943 and the plan was to use Auschwitz-Birkenau to eliminate the rest of Europe's Jewry. Extra barracks and larger luggage sorting facilities were added while a railway line was laid right into the centre of the camp.

Prisoners underwent selection on the Birkenau train ramp, with the elderly, the young, the infirm and the sick being sent straight to the gas chambers. Those deemed fit enough to work were held in the barracks until one of the twenty-eight subcamps in the area called for more labourers. A Zone of Interest covering forty square kilometres had been growing at the same rate as the camps. A huge chemical works run by IG Farben was being built at nearby Monowitz (Monowice in Polish) while other factories, mines, quarries and farms were expanding.

Altogether four crematoria were built and they went into operation between March and June 1943. It has been estimated that they could murder 4,700 people every day and dispose of their bodies; 140,000 a month. Auschwitz-Birkenau was achieving three objectives: employing workers on site, sending labourers to other camps, and murdering those unable to work. Eventually over 65,000 workers would be employed in the Concentration Camp Zone.

Liebehenschel had replaced Höss in November 1943 but he returned in May 1944 to supervise Special Action Hungary, the gassing of the Hungarian Jews; the camp's deadliest period. The last trainload of Jews arrived on 30 October and the dismantling of the crematoria started around the same time.

Red Army troops entered the ruins of Warsaw on 17 January 1945 as the remaining staff burnt the camp's paperwork. Extra guards arrived to escort 58,000 prisoners out of the Concentration Camp Zone and those too weak to move were murdered. Around 10,000 would die from the cold, hunger and the guards' brutality during the long march across the Third Reich. Many ended up in Bergen-Belsen, where many succumbed to the typhus epidemic ravaging the overwhelmed camp.

Attempts were made to remove every scrap of evidence of the gas chambers, but Red Army soldiers discovered the ruins as well as huts filled with clothing and human hair on 27 January 1945. They also found hundreds of emaciated prisoners who had been abandoned by their guards. The Soviets reported the camp to be the ultimate capitalist factory in which the prisoners were just some of many 'victims of fascism'. It was a view which remained until the fall of communism.

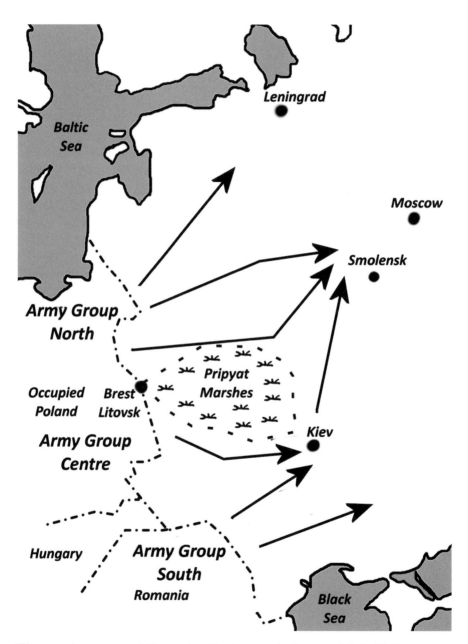

The opening stages of Operation Barbarossa in June and July 1941.

Chapter 14

The Battle for Poland

Operation Barbarossa and the Polish People's Army

After the trials of the combined Nazi and Soviet invasion and repression, Poland endured two more huge battles before the end of the war. The first was the largest military operation in history: Operation Barbarossa, which was launched by the Wehrmacht on 22 June 1941. The second military campaign was spread out between the spring of 1944 and the beginning of 1945, as the Red Army advanced across what had once been Poland to the gates of Berlin. This book focuses on the Polish aspect. It covers the early stages of the Wehrmacht's advance across Poland's eastern territories, known as the Kresy. It then covers the part played by Polish People's Army, which served under the Red Army.

Operation Barbarossa

By the spring of 1941 over 675,000 German troops had gathered in Poland's eastern territories. A similar number of troops were assembled in Romanian's eastern region. They were poised to make the largest attack in military history and its codename would be Barbarossa. The original date was set for 15 May and the Luftwaffe flew surveillance missions over Soviet territory while diversions called Operations Shark and Harpoon made it look as though Britain and Norway were about to be invaded.

Zero hour was eventually delayed to 22 June 1941 and several theories have been put forward as to why. Some believe the decision to invade Yugoslavia in April 1941 tied up vital resources. Others say that Finland and Romania needed extra time to prepare their attacks to the north and south of the Wehrmacht. Various sources think that the rivers and streams remained in flood until the late spring, making it impossible to use the primitive roads.

Whatever the reason, the Wehrmacht had assembled 104 infantry divisions, 19 panzer divisions and 15 motorized infantry divisions in three army groups by mid-June 1941. Another four German and fourteen Finnish divisions were poised to attack across the Finnish border while thirteen Romanian divisions were ready on the southern flank. Nine security divisions composed of Waffen-SS and *Einsatzgruppen* would follow up the advance and secure the conquered territories with their terror tactics. The divisions were gathered in four Army Groups:

Army Norway would attack across the Finnish border.

Army Group North would advance through the Baltic States.

Army Group Centre would cross Belorussia.

Army Group South would move through the Ukraine.

The Wehrmacht had assembled 3.8 million personnel and 3,500 tanks and they were supported by three large Luftwaffe fleets.

The Red Army was the polar opposite of the Wehrmacht. The recent purge had resulted in 30,000 officers, many of them experienced and senior staff, being murdered. The State Defence Plan and Mobilisation Plan called for 171 divisions to be ready to meet an invasion, while another 57 divisions would be ready soon afterwards. It meant that the Soviet Union had to put nearly 5.5 million men into the field and there were shortages of every type of equipment, in particular transport. The Red Army had 14,700 tanks on paper, but they were dispersed across the front line, rather than being deployed in battle groups. All were lacking adequate communications, maintenance and supply units. The Soviet Air Force could put 19,500 aircraft into the air but, again, most were deployed near the border.

Stalin had ignored several warnings from Britain about an impending attack, believing that Prime Minister Winston Churchill was trying to trick him into becoming his ally. As we have seen, the date of the attack had been postponed, so he treated the new date with some suspicion. He had also shied away from deploying too many troops along the border, so as not to provoke Hitler into making an attack.

The attack, which was made early on 22 June 1941, came as a surprise to Stalin and his generals. Rudimentary communication systems and savage attacks against the Red Army command and control structure meant that it took several hours to pass on messages. Some units had already been overrun or surrounded by the time they received Stalin's order to counter-attack against what he referred to as border violations.

Joseph Goebbels declared, 'At this moment a march is taking place that compares with the greatest the world has ever seen. I have decided today to place the fate and future of the Reich and our people in the hands of our soldiers. May God aid us, especially in this fight!' Nazi Germany would later refer to Operation Barbarossa as a 'European crusade against Bolshevism'.

The air campaign was a decisive success: the Luftwaffe knocked out nearly 1,500 planes in the first hours, many of them on the ground, crippling the Soviet Air Force; an equal number would be put out of action over the days that followed. Army Group North broke through the Red Army defences in Lithuania and then easily stopped the Red Army counter-attacks. It reached the Dvina River in Latvia after just three days, forcing the Red Army to withdraw to the Stalin Line which protected Leningrad. Army Group Centre's two panzer groups bypassed Brest Fortress and drove quickly across Belarus, bypassing the north side of the Pripyat marshes, as it captured Minsk en route to Smolensk. They captured around 324,000 men, 3,300 tanks and 1,800 artillery pieces as the NKVD and Soviet commissars used force to stop the civilians panicking. General Dmitry Pavlov would be relieved and he and many of his staff were shot for cowardice and incompetence.

Army Group South had been split into two halves and the northern group faced tough opposition as it advanced between the Pripyat marshes and the Carpathian Mountains. It had stopped a number of counter-attacks by the time the Red Army withdrew to the Stalin Line, to defend Kiev. The southern group delayed its invasion of Moldavia until 2 July invaded and it then advanced north-east towards the River Dniester, looking to take Kiev from the south.

By the beginning of July, the Wehrmacht had driven the Red Army from the Kresy, at the beginning of the long advance which would take it to the gates of Leningrad, Moscow and Stalingrad. The fighting might have been brief, except at a few fortresses like Brest Litovsk, but the *Einsatzgruppen* were close behind the combat units. Before long, they were executing the remaining Polish intelligentsia and rounding up the Jews, either to shoot in the woods or hold inside ghettos.

The Red Army Advances

After all the trials under the Nazis, the people of Poland faced a new threat when the Wehrmacht fell back in the face of increasing attacks by the Red Army. The fighting would rage across what had been Polish territory between the spring of 1944 and the beginning of 1945. Polish men in the

Soviet Army fought in the battles for their own country while civilians died in the fighting. The Home Army rose up, hoping to hasten the Germany army's departure and seize their country. Meanwhile, both left-and right-wing political groups were eyeing up control of post-war Poland.

The Polish People's Army

Operation Barbarossa resulted in the Government-in-Exile and Moscow talking again after the fall out over the Katyń massacre. General Władysław Sikorski and Ivan Mayski signed a pact in July 1941 under which the Soviet Union cancelled all pacts with Nazi Germany. Stalin agreed to an amnesty for Polish citizens and to release all Polish prisoners of war (omitting that fact that 20,000 officers had been executed at Katyń). Around 40,000 soldiers were organised under General Anders: they headed for Iran and eventually joined the fight in the Mediterranean.

The Red Army started to drive the Wehrmacht back after the battle of Stalingrad and they coerced Polish men into joining the Red Army, until the Polish People's Army was the size of an army corps. But the Germans had discovered the massacre site in the Katyń Wood and the resulting arguments ended in diplomatic relations between Moscow and the Government-in-Exile being severed.

The Battle of Lenino

The Polish armed forces' first major battle was part of the Spas-Demensk offensive, in the autumn of 1943. The 1st Tadeusz Kościuszko Infantry Division and the 1st Polish Tank Regiment had to break through the Panther-Wotan defences but most of the men were conscripts who had enlisted to escape the Gulag camps.

Some of General Zygmunt Berling's men deserted as they probed the Mereya River, north of Lenino, on 9 October 1943. The rest of the Poles attacked on 12 October, only to discover that their enemy had abandoned their first line of defence before the bombardment started. It left the infantry in a salient without tank support and an improvised barrage was needed to stop the German counter-attack.

The Red Army commander, Vasily Gordov, ordered the Poles to make another attempt, but Berling went above his head to ask for the order to be cancelled because it would be suicidal. Unfortunately the second attack was made before he was given an answer. The 1st Division had secured a bridgehead but at a terrible cost, and it would be six months before it was fit to return to the front line. Lenino would be used as a jumping-off position at the start of Operation Bagration in June 1944.

The Advance across Poland

The name of the Polish People's Army was changed to the Armed Forces of the Republic of Poland in March 1944 while the 1st Tadeusz Kościuszko Division was reorganised into the First Polish Army, under General Zygmunt Berling. It had 30,000 soldiers but all the commanders, all the political officers and half the military officers were Soviet.

First Army crossed the old Polish border with the First Belorussian Front in the summer of 1944 as part of Operation Bagration. It advanced west across the Vistula, seventy miles south of Warsaw, but was then moved north. The Poles made a late attempt to relieve the Home Army units fighting for their lives in the city, but they were too few and too late to help.

The Vistula-Oder Offensive

The Red Army had assembled 2.2 million troops, 7,000 tanks, 13,750 artillery pieces and 5,000 aircraft while Army Group A only had 450,000 soldiers, 1,150 tanks and 4,100 artillery pieces to stop them. Marshal Georgy Zhukov and Marshal Ivan Konev already had bridgeheads over the Vistula, south of Warsaw, and the attack started on 12 January. The First Belorussian Front broke out of the Puławy and Magnuszew bridgeheads, and part of it headed west towards Radom while the rest closed in on Warsaw. The Poles took control of the ruins of Warsaw by 17 January and then helped break through Germany's pre-war border defences, known as the Pomeranian Wall. After taking Łódź there was a fight for Poznań, while the rest of First Army drove north to the Baltic coast, cutting off Army Group Centre. Around 5,000 Poles were killed or injured during the fight for Fortress Kolberg in March. The survivors then held a 'wedding to the sea' ceremony which symbolised Poland once again getting access to the Baltic coast. Meanwhile the First Ukrainian Front had pushed west from the Vistula at Sandomierz, bypassing Kraków as the Germans withdrew from the industrial region of Silesia.

The Red Army had advanced 300 miles to the River Oder in just two weeks. The Soviet troops were only fifty miles from Berlin, and while there were no troops to defend the capital, Zhukov had to clear Pomerania first before he could push further west. The Poles' final battle involved nearly 75,000 men fighting their way past the north side of Berlin. They then had to stop German counter-attacks which tried to relieve the city's garrison.

The Nazis had evacuated their concentration camps ahead of the Red Army advance and 250,000 men and women were forced to walk west in severe winter weather in what became known as the 'Death Marches'. Auschwitz was just one of the concentration camps to be liberated on 27 January but, as in most cases, a lot of evidence relating to the atrocities had been removed or destroyed. The rapid advance of the Red Army frightened the ethnic Germans; over 800,000 moved into Poland, encouraged by anti-Soviet propaganda distributed by the Nazis.

The Second Polish Army and the Battle of Bautzen, April 1945

The Polish Second Army had deployed on the First Ukrainian Front's southern flank in January 1945. It broke the German defences and had crossed the River Spree, north of Bautzen, on 17 April. The Red Army was securing Bautzen, so General Karol Świerczewski decided to advance towards Dresden, contrary to Marshal Konev's plan. The Fourth Panzer Army counter-attacked the over-extended Second Polish Army on 21 April, overrunning many units. Red Army divisions moved up to help but one division and a tank brigade had been destroyed by the time the line had stabilised.

Świerczewski renewed the advance towards Dresden on 26 April, only to find that the Fourth Panzer Army had reinforced the area. Again the Poles were badly mauled as military units and refugees escaped towards Dresden. Altogether the Polish Second Army suffered over twenty per cent casualties and lost half their tanks in one of the last German counter-attacks of the war.

Second Army then switched its line of attack to the south, heading for Prague. By the end of the war the Red Army had a considerable number of Polish units in its ranks. There were ten infantry divisions, a tank corps, eight artillery brigades and a range of supporting arms.

The Polish People's Air Force

The Soviets started forming a Polish Air Force in July 1943. The 1st Independent Fighter Squadron expanded into the 1st Fighter Regiment (Warsaw) and was joined by the 2nd Bomber Regiment (Kraków) and the 103rd Independent Liaison Aviation Squadron in April 1944. Around 600 Poles started training at Soviet aviation schools and Colonel Józef Smaga had organised one hundred aircraft into the 1st Air Force Division on August 1944. Fighter pilots flew the fast and manoeuvrable Yakovlev Yak-1 while the bomber pilots flew the Ilyushin Il-2 ground-attack aircraft, nicknamed the 'Flying Tank' because of its heavy armour. A liaison squadron flew Polikarpov Po-2 biplanes.

The fighter pilots first flew in support of the First Polish Army during the Lublin-Brest Offensive at the end of August 1944, the bomber pilots made their first raid on 11 September. Polish pilots also flew around 600 flights over Warsaw during the six-week long uprising, either attacking German positions or dropping supplies.

The 1st Air Force Division was renamed the 4th Mixed Air Force Division when the Polish I Mixed Air Force Corps was formed in September 1944. Polish staff replaced the Soviet personnel as soon as they had finished their training and they were equipped with over 300 new aircraft, which were faster and more manoeuvrable. They included Yak-3 and Yak-9 fighters and Petlyakov Pe-2 ground attack aircraft.

The Polish Army Air Force Command was formed in October 1944 and Major General Teodor Połynin deployed in support of the First Polish Army at the end of the year. Pilots flew hundreds of flights during the advance from the Vistula and Oder rivers through Berlin to the Elbe over the next four months. Combat missions were finally stopped on 4 May to prevent incidents with American combat planes. The Polish pilots had flown around 5,800 combat flights in nine months.

The Home Army Strikes Back

The Polish underground made plans to attack German rear area units and seize the cities across the General Government during the winter of 1942-3. The idea was to form sixteen infantry divisions and several cavalry brigades with existing members and to add a similar number organised from volunteers. They planned to ambush units withdrawing from the Red Army in the hope that it would show the Soviets that they deserved to rule their own country again.

The brutal battle for Stalingrad made it clear that Hitler was going to make the Wehrmacht fight for every mile of territory, so General Rowecki scaled down the uprising:

1. The Fan (*Wachlarz*) sabotage units would attack the German supply lines in the north

2. There would be uprisings east of the Vistula, in the centre
3. Further uprisings west of the river

Matters took a turn for the worse following the news of the Katyń massacre, because the Government-in-Exile cut diplomatic ties with Moscow on 25 April 1943. Rowecki was still hopeful that the Home Army would be able to help. The Red Army crossed Poland's pre-war border at the beginning of 1944 and the Home Army launched Operation Tempest soon afterwards. Units came out of hiding to attack the Wehrmacht's rear echelons and while they cooperated with the advancing Red Army units, it was soon clear what their true intentions were.

Local Soviet commanders welcomed any help from the Poles until the fighting was over and then they were told to lay down their arms and split into officers and other ranks. The officers were interrogated and those with anti-Soviet views were imprisoned or shot. The rest joined the other ranks who had been enlisted into the Red Army, rather than being deported to a labour camp.

The Warsaw Uprising, 1 August to 2 October 1944

Warsaw was always considered a thorn in the Germans' side because of the high number of assassinations and acts of sabotage. The city was considered such a risk that Hans Frank decided to base the headquarters of the General Government in Kraków. In December 1943 he wrote,

Warsaw is the one place in this country which is a source of all our misfortunes. We would not have four-fifths of the troubles we are facing now without Warsaw. It is the focus of all disturbances and the place from which discontent is spread through the whole country.

The Home Army had been considering what to do since the Red Army crossed the pre-1939 Polish border on 13 July 1943. They might antagonise the Soviets if they attacked the German rear but they could be called cowards or collaborators if they did nothing. General Tadeusz Komorowski started discussing what to do in November 1943 with the rest of the Home Army commanders, and they came up with the compromise which would be codenamed Operation Tempest.

Home Army units would attack the Germans as they withdrew, sometimes cooperating with Red Army units, and it seemed that the plan was working to begin with. However, there was soon news that the NKVD were executing some Home Army officers and conscripting everyone else into the Red Army. So it was time to take drastic action. The Government-in-Exile had given Komorowski permission to stage a general uprising, even though Sosnkowski, Sikorski's recent replacement, disapproved of the plan.

The failed assassination of Hitler by a conspiracy of German generals on 20 July 1944 coincided with the Red Army closing in on Warsaw. A week later Governor Ludwig Fischer put out an order calling for 100,000 civilians to fortify the ruins, but few volunteered. Komorowski knew that round-ups would follow and he did not want his soldiers to be put to work when they could be fighting.

Radio Kosciuszko (named after the 18th century Polish national hero) transmitted messages from Moscow calling for the people of Warsaw to rise up as the Red Army closed in on Warsaw. So Komorowski told the Home Army commanders that Explosion Hour or *Wybuch* Hour would be at 5 pm on 1 August.

Colonel Antoni Chruściel (codename the Fitter) had between 20,000 and 50,000 soldiers to call on, divided into eight commands. They would be joined by several thousand men belonging to smaller partisan groups, including many Jews who were released from Gęsiówka concentration camp at the beginning of the uprising. They wore a mixture of uniforms and civilian clothing but they all wore the red-white armband of the national flag. They also believed in their motto, that they were fighting 'for ours and for your freedom'.

While they had a desire to defeat the Germans, they lacked the weapons to do so because many had been sent to other cities to arm those staging other uprisings. The defenders of Warsaw had only 2,750 single shot weapons, 350 automatic weapons, 25,000 hand grenades and 20 anti-tank guns. Brave men would capture a few German armoured vehicles in the early days, while valiant pilots flew supply missions over the city later in the siege.

Governor Ludwig Fischer suspected something was about to happen, so he alerted the city's military commanders on 1 August. General Rainer Stahel's called out the 11,000-strong Warsaw garrison while Colonel Paul Otto Geibel raised around 5,700 members of the Security Police and Waffen-SS. They would be supported by tanks, all manner of artillery and rocket launchers, and aircraft. The warning was also put to all sorts of paramilitary and party units.

The Home Army captured most of the city centre and the old town but they failed to take the university, Castle Square, the German headquarters in the Saxon Palace, or the PAST tower. They also failed to seize the citadel and the railway station, so many soldiers headed into the forests north of the city. There was success in the Wola district but there were too few troops to take control of the countryside west of the city. They could not capture the SS and Sipo barracks in the Ochota district, nor the Mokotów police headquarters in the south of the city. But the ghetto area and Gęsiówka concentration camp were eventually captured and many of the Jewish prisoners grabbed a weapon and joined the fight against the Germans. The Germans held onto Okęcie and Mokotów airfields in the south half of the city and many of the Poles again headed into the forests to regroup. German units also held onto the bridges across the Vistula, cutting off the units fighting in Praga on the east bank.

The Germans took their time to identify which city blocks the Home Army units were holding before moving in to split the Home Army units up. SS-General Erich von dem Bach took command of the situation on 4 August and his troops started fighting their way through the Wola and Ochota districts on the west side of the city. They had to remove road blocks made of paving stones and cut through barbed wire as they cleared fortified buildings, bunkers and cellars. The Home Army fought back fiercely with their small arms but the Germans was backed by tanks, artillery, rocket launchers and dive bombers. They often resorted to using flame throwers to clear rooms, explosives to bring down walls, and fire hoses to flood cellars.

SS-Gruppenführer Heinz Reinefarth deployed execution squads to mop up behind the advancing troops and they showed no mercy. Everyone, men, women and children, was considered to be a partisan and as many as 100,000 soldiers and civilians were executed. News of the massacres made the Poles realise there could be no surrender and no escape; they would have to fight to the last bullet.

Tanks supported the infantry as they fought their way into the centre of the city, sometimes forcing civilians to walk in front of them as human shields. They cleared Bankowy Plaza, cutting off the Wola district, and then fought their way through the Old Town, linking up groups of German troops en route to the River Vistula.

Bach organised his troops into two battle groups, led by SS-Gruppenführer Reinefarth and SS-Brigadeführer Günter Rohr, on 20 August. They included the RONA Brigade, composed of bloodthirsty collaborators from the Russian National Liberation Army. A renewed attack then forced the Home Army back, because they were running out of ammunition, and many withdrew through the sewers to new positions. The fighting had degenerated into a stalemate by the time Himmler commented on the battle: 'This is the fiercest of our battles since the start of the war. It compares to the street battles of Stalingrad.'

Colonel Chruściel was promoted as he reorganised his remaining troops into the Warsaw Home Army Corps. He grouped them into three divisions, naming them after the areas they held: the Żoliborz Division in the north, the Śródmieście Division in the centre and the Mokotów Division in the south. Throughout the fighting, the Home Army had appealed to the Red Army to advance the short distance to the Praga district on the east bank of the Vistula. That would have divided the Germans' attention and given the Poles a better chance of winning their battle on the west bank. But Stalin had wanted the Home Army to exhaust itself first, making it easier to eliminate the organisation in the future.

A Red Army offensive eventually began on 26 August, but it took the understrength First Polish Army over two weeks to drive the Germans back to the Vistula. Patrols contacted the Home Army on 14 September and a bridgehead was formed, but the relief force was too weak to push into the city. Soviet High Command refused to provide any reinforcements but they still blamed General Berling for the failure and he was relieved. After a five-day battle, only a few Poles escaped across the river and the relief attempt was called off. It had cost the First Polish Army over 5,500 casualties.

The one million civilians living in Warsaw had not been warned about the uprising, so they had not stockpiled any food. The prolonged fighting meant that supplies soon ran out and many survived on a weak brew called 'spit-soup', made from ground barley and boiled water. The explosions and demolitions had smashed many water pipes while the Germans blew up the city's pumping stations to cut off the remaining water supply. Many Poles were reduced to digging in their backyards in the hope of finding water.

The situation for civilians in the Home Army-held area deteriorated rapidly. Komorowski and Rohr agreed that 20,000 civilians could be given safe passage out of the war-torn city. Rohr also agreed that Home Army soldiers would be treated as prisoners of war, in the hope that they would surrender rather than fight to the death.

The Home Army's Bureau of Information and Propaganda despatched film crews during the first hours of the uprising and they recorded the seizure of key buildings and the return of normal life in some areas. Daily newspapers and information sheets kept the citizens of Warsaw informed, while a radio transmitter started broadcasting news and patriotic messages, starting on 7 August. They also sent appeals to the Red Army, looking for military help; they were ignored.

A Lack of Assistance and Surrender

The Royal Air Force, the Polish Air Force and the South African Air Force started dropping supplies over Warsaw as early as 4 August, but it was difficult to spot the flares marking the landing zones amongst the burning buildings. The Soviet Union banned the pilots from landing on their airfields for several weeks, forcing them into a long, dangerous flight from either Britain or Italy.

Eventually Moscow relented and one hundred B-17 Flying Fortresses started Operation Frantic on 18 September. American pilots flew over the city and dropped their loads before refuelling and making another supply drop on the journey home. The problem was that the Home Army had been pushed into small areas and it was even more difficult to find the drop zones. Then after only three days, the Soviets closed their airfields, only opening them againwhen the weather turned bad. It was if they were trying to stop the Western Allies from helping.

The Soviet Air Force would fly over 2,500 supply missions. But they did not start until six weeks into the battle. The small Polikarpov Po-2 biplanes could not carry much and many canisters smashed on the ground as they had no parachutes.

The Red Army's crossing of the River Narew to the north of Warsaw and the Vistula to the south convinced the Home Army leaders to start their uprising. Soviet troops were only a few miles from the east side of Warsaw and it was expected that they could break through the German line in a matter of days and link up with the Polish-held area in the centre of the city.

Stalin had other ideas because he was looking at the long-term future of a communist Poland. He did not want the Polish partisans running their country; he wanted them in prison or dead. The Kremlin halted Forty Seventh Army only six miles from Warsaw as soon as it heard about the uprising. It would not move for forty-one days. Stalin told a puzzled Churchill that the halt was due to a setback which he wanted to keep secret. When Stalin finally allowed it to, Forty Seventh Army easily cleared the Praga suburb along the east bank of the Vistula.

The Germans accused the Soviets of abandoning the Poles, and they were right. Stalin had even gone as far as ordering the Red Army to stop all

Home Army units from reaching Warsaw. He wanted the Polish partisans and their leaders to die in a one-sided battle for their capital.

The surrender was signed on 2 October, after the Wehrmacht promised to treat the Home Army soldiers as prisoners of war, and over 15,000 Polish partisans were marched into camps. They also said they would look after the civilian population once the guns fell silent, and over half a million were sent to a transit camp in Pruszków, five miles south-west of the city. Around 5,000 partisans were hidden among them. The civilians were interviewed and while around 90,000 were sent to labour camps to work, 60,000 were deemed to be dangerous and sent to extermination or concentration camps to die. The rest were sent on trains into the General Government and released.

Himmler was furious that the people of Warsaw had dared to rise up and was determined to make sure the Poles never tried again. He announced, 'The city must completely disappear from the surface of the earth and serve only as a transport station for the Wehrmacht. No stone can remain standing. Every building must be razed to its foundation.' So German engineers set about systematically blowing up every structure they could find, whether it was intact or ruined. Nine out of ten buildings lay in ruins by the time the Red Army entered the city on 17 January 1945. Over ten thousand structures, including the city's fine historical and cultural centres, were destroyed. It left over one million people homeless, with nothing more than what they could carry.

Other Home Army Uprisings

Lieutenant Colonel Aleksander Krzyżanowski (codename Wolf) planned to stage an uprising on 8 July 1944 as the Red Army approached Wilno (Vilnius). Unfortunately he had to launch Operation Dawn Gate twenty-four hours early because the Soviet troops were moving faster than anticipated. It meant that most of the units did not have time to mobilise, and the few attacks were ineffective.

The Soviets and Polish fought their way side-by-side through Wilno for several days and Krzyżanowski's men ambushed the Germans as they abandoned the city on 13 July. General Ivan Czerniachowski initially promised Krzyżanowski that his men would be given arms and equipment, and then arrested him. His men dispersed into the forests but the Soviets had soon tracked down 5,500 of them. They were either conscripted or sent to the Gulag.

The German soldiers and their Ukrainian paramilitaries began leaving Lwów as the Red Army approached on 18 July 1944. Colonel Władysław Filipkowski (codename Cis or Janka) postponed a coup to take control of the city when more German soldiers arrived, but decided to go on the offensive when the Soviets began attacking three days later. Home Army units cleared areas of the city, sometimes with the help of Soviet tanks, as the Wehrmacht withdrew through the city. Many of Filipkowski's men were imprisoned or conscripted into the Soviet Army when the fighting was over; the rest went into hiding.

Home Army units engaged the Germans north and east of Brest-Litovsk as they withdrew ahead of the Soviet offensive called Operation Bagration. They contacted the Red Army on 30 July 1944 but refused to join the First Polish Army. Instead they planned to head for Warsaw, where the uprising had just started, only to find themselves surrounded and disarmed by the Red Army.

Large partisan actions by infantry and cavalry were carried out in the forests of what had been north-east Poland. However, the sizeable German garrisons in Augustow, Grodno and Białystok made it too dangerous to enter the cities.

A month later, the Home Army, the National Military Organisation and the People's Army worked together to disrupt the Wehrmacht's supply lines around Lublin. Over 30,000 soldiers were deployed with tank, artillery and air support as part of Operation Hurricane I, and they surrounded 3,000 partisans in the Janów Forest. Many escaped the largest partisan battle of the war, only to become trapped in the Solska Wilderness when the Germans launched Operation Hurricane II. This time, the Polish and Soviet commanders disagreed over what to do and hardly any of their men escaped.

Three Home Army divisions seized bridgeheads along the Vistula between Sandomierz and Magnuszew, when the uprising started in Warsaw to the north on 1 August. They held them until the Red Army arrived on 14 August 1944 and then General Komorowski decided to reinforce the uprising in Warsaw under the codename Operation Revenge. Colonel Jan Zientarski (codename Farmer) led 6,500 soldiers north, only to find too many German troops around the city, so they dispersed.

Thousands of partisans armed themselves around Kraków and Przemyśl, ready to rise up as the Red Army approached. However, disaster struck when many key members were arrested in round-ups on 6 August which had been organised as revenge for the Warsaw Uprising. Colonel Edward Godlewski abandoned the idea to stage an uprising on 10 October, following protests from Archbishop Adam Sapieha. His men had too few weapons to defeat the large number of soldiers garrisoning the capital of the General Government and he wanted to avoid atrocities like those committed in Warsaw.

Post-War Memories

The story of the Home Army's battles was a problem for the communists after the war. Many wanted to remember the uprisings but the communists wanted to forget them. The People's Republic of Poland generally ignored it, occasionally blaming the military failure and the civilian massacres on the Government-in-Exile and the Home Army. It also banned adverse comments about the Red Army's actions, particularly its half-hearted attempt to help the partisans in Warsaw.

Stories were allowed to circulate in the 1950s, but the party line was to blame the Home Army's officers for the military failure and to portray the soldiers as the heroes. Meanwhile, exiles spread honest stories of heroism wherever they settled in the west. Memories of the Warsaw Uprising would eventually become commonplace in Poland in the 1980s, because they inspired the labour movement, Solidarity, to oppose the communist government with another type of rebellion. It was, however, 1989 (forty-five years after the uprising) before the first Home Army monument was dedicated.

It is believed that 16,000 members of the Home Army and other partisan groups were killed during the uprising while another 6,000 badly wounded soldiers were taken prisoner. Another 200,000 Polish civilians lost their lives, the vast majority of them executed. German casualties were estimated at 8,000 killed and 9,000 wounded. Operation Tempest was called off at the end of the month and all units were dissolved.

The Political Battle

The Polish Patriots' Union was formed in June 1943 as a political and social group for Poles living in the Soviet Union. It proved to be an important link in the wake of the news of the Katyń Massacre, and the president, Wanda Wasilewska, said the Government-in-Exile was an obstacle to the 'Anglo-Russo–American block'. The Union was dominated by communists and it wanted to implement Stalinism in Poland as soon as the Nazis had been driven out.

The Polish Workers' Party had formed the State National Council in Warsaw on 31 December 1943 and Władysław Gomułka's council declared the Government-in-Exile illegitimate and challenged the actions of the Polish Underground State. Bolesław Bierut was sent from the Soviet Union to be the council chairman, and while he argued with Gomułka, the State National Council was accepted and then supported by Moscow. The People's Army was its armed force and it carried out sabotage attacks against the Germans separate from the Home Army.

The State National Council, the Patriots' Union and the Workers' Party established the National Liberation Committee in July 1944, to continue challenging the Government-in-Exile's claim that they represented the Polish people. Stalin approved the communist members, and while Edward Osóbka-Morawski was the chairman he was guided by the Soviet representative Nikolai Bulganin and the NKVD general Ivan Serov. The committee relocated from Moscow to Lublin and was usually referred to as the Lublin Committee.

The unelected group started governing the areas of Poland cleared by the Red Army under Moscow's guidance, but it caused friction between the United Nations and the Soviet Union. The committee called for the 1921 constitution to be reintroduced because it believed the 1935 version was fascist. But it also wanted land reform, collectivisation and for Poland's borders to move west, so the Soviet Union could take over the Kresy.

Winston Churchill and the Polish Prime Minister in exile Stanisław Mikołajczyk flew to Moscow as the Red Army advanced across Poland in the summer of 1944. They were both worried that the Soviet Union wanted to annex Poland's eastern territories, which they had occupied in September 1939. Over 11.5 million people lived in the huge area and one in three were ethnic Poles. Stalin was adamant that the Kresy should be added to Lithuania, Belorussia and the Ukraine while Poland received the eastern part of Germany in return. He also suggested that the exiled government could join the Soviet-sponsored Polish Committee of National Liberation.

The State National Council renamed the National Liberation Committee the Provisional Government of the Republic of Poland on 31 December 1944. It continued to oppose the Government-in-Exile, and while there were protests from the Western Allies, Stalin planned to keep Poland under Soviet rule.

The Committee was again chaired by Osóbka-Morawski but General Serov still kept a close eye on its business. It relocated to Warsaw when the city was captured in January 1945 and it then waited for the outcome of the Yalta Conference in the Crimea, hearing that Stalin promised 'free and unfettered elections'.

General Serov invited members of the Government Delegation, the Council of National Unity and the Home Army commander-in-chief to the Soviet Union in the spring of 1945. He wanted to grant them places in the Soviet Provisional Government and offered them a guarantee for their safety. All sixteen were arrested not long after they arrived in Moscow and were interrogated in the NKVD's dreaded headquarters, the Lubyanka.

They were put on trial in June 1945, and while Lieutenant General Vasili Ulrikh found twelve guilty of many crimes, three of them were acquitted. London and Washington DC protested on behalf of the Government-in-Exile but Moscow said their sentences would not be long. Three would die in captivity, ten would survive their sentences but two of them would be forced to emigrate.

The Provisional Government of the Republic of Poland would be renamed the Provisional Government of National Unity on 28 June 1945.

NIE (Niepodległość) or Independence

In September 1943 the Polish Government-in-Exile decided it wanted to organise an anti-Soviet campaign before the Red Army crossed the Polish border. General Sosnkowski (codenames included Shepherd, Richard and the Chief) coordinated the British activities while General Komorowski (codename Forest) chose the people to carry it out across Poland. The plan was to form self-defence groups to protect civilians, distribute anti-Soviet propaganda and to track the Red Army's advance.

General Leopold Okulicki (codename Cobra or Bear) was appointed to lead the campaign in May 1944 but Operation Tempest interfered with it before much could be done. Many members then became involved in the Warsaw Uprising in August; they were either killed or captured. Okulicki tried in vain to restart the campaign in Poland's eastern territories, so he met General Emil Fieldorf (codename Nil) in January 1945 to coordinate NIE's activities with the Home Army.

Unfortunately both Okulicki and Fieldorf were arrested by the NKVD, accused of anti-Soviet activities, two months later. Okulicki was murdered in a Moscow prison in December 1946 while Fieldorf was executed in a Warsaw prison in 1953. Colonel Antoni Sanojca took over NIE and had closed it down by the end of the war.

General Anders formed the Armed Forces Delegation for Poland on 7 May 1945, to take over where the disbanded NIE organisation had left off. Colonel Jan Rzepecki organised it like the Home Army, and while the plan was to deploy troops to fight the communists, it was replaced by the Freedom and Independence organisation on 8 August 1945.

Location of the Home Army uprisings in the summer of 1944.

Chapter 15

Sabotage and Uprising

The Underground State and the Home Army

The Underground State

Himmler acknowledged the extent to which the various underground groups were affecting the German war effort in December 1942:

> *The intelligence service of the Polish resistance movement has assumed major significance within the framework of the entire enemy intelligence operations directed against Germany. Major police security operations have discovered the scale and importance of the resistance operations and how they have been skilfully delegated down to the smallest splinter group.*

The Underground State's political arm, the Political Consultative Committee, was renamed the Home Political Representation in August 1943. It recognised the Government-in-Exile and representatives from the four major political parties represented on the Government Delegation, Poland's provisional government.

The politicians secretly prepared to resume running the country, once the war was over. They organised a judiciary and courts to sentence Nazi and Soviet war criminals. The Underground State recruited pre-war police officers into the State Security Corps and the Local Government Guard to make criminal investigations against the occupying forces. Marian Kozielewski (codename Konrad) had seen the organisations grow to 12,000 members by the time he was injured during the Warsaw Uprising; Stanisław Tabisz (codename Tank) then took over the gathering of intelligence on members of the Gestapo and the Criminal Police. The Directorate of Civil Resistance instructed the Special Courts to give its verdict on those accused of war crimes. The Directorate of Underground Resistance then considered what action to take and their decision often resulted in an assassination attempt.

The Underground State also ran schools, held cultural events and produced publications. The Nazis were determined to turn the Poles into uneducated manual workers, but hundreds of teachers risked their lives to organise underground schools as part of the Secret Teaching Organisation. They taught forbidden subjects on Polish history and culture to thousands of children to secondary school level and some even to university level. Members of the Home Army ran underground schools to teach military skills, and members of the Church ran secret courses on religious studies. The Archbishop of Kraków, Cardinal Adam Sapieha, trained Karol Wojtyla, who would become Pope John Paul II in 1978.

The Underground State opened offices across the country which copied the pre-war local authorities, only their priorities were different. They would serve the people by attacking the Nazis or by defending them from the occupying forces. The preparations for a post-war democratic state would eventually employ around 15,000 people.

Poland was placed under the Soviet sphere of influence at the Tehran Conference (28 November 1943), even though no Polish representatives were invited to argue the nation's case. Stalin believed that the Government-in-Exile did not represent Polish interests and neither Roosevelt nor Churchill objected to his point of view. So he returned to Moscow to create a Soviet-controlled puppet government which could take control of areas liberated by the Red Army.

The Home Political Representation was unable to come to any agreement with the Soviet-backed Polish Workers Party, so it had to reinvent itself as the National Unity Council under Kazimierz Pużak in January 1944, to counter the new communist State National Council. It also published a document entitled 'What is the Polish Nation Fighting For?' which argued for a democratic state, with equality for minorities, freedom of speech and the right to practise all religious and political ideas. It wanted land reform, the nationalisation of industry and a redistribution of income. The document also called for territorial compensation from Germany and reinstatement of the country's pre-1939 eastern border.

Three months later the Government-in-Exile recognised the importance of the Delegate's Office in Warsaw. It made it the Temporary Government in Poland and gave it permission to form a Council of Ministers at Home. It also appointed Pużak as deputy to Prime Minister Stanisław Mikołajczyk, who was based in London. But the National Liberation Committee was established in Lublin in July 1944 to rival their claim and its political takeover of eastern Poland was recognised by all. Meanwhile the

Government-in-Exile was losing favour and it would eventually be referred to as an 'illegal and self-styled authority'. The Temporary Government in Poland also lost influence, because the Home Army suffered many casualties during Operation Tempest and the Warsaw Uprising.

Prime Minister Mikołajczyk resigned in November 1944 and his replacement, Tomasz Arciszewski, was ineffective at fighting the Government-in-Exile's case. Again, no Polish representatives were invited to the Yalta Conference in February 1945 where it was agreed that the Lublin-based government was a temporary solution. Poland would have an election, albeit a rigged one, as soon as the war was over, but many Poles thought they had been betrayed.

The Government Delegate's Office at Home (meaning in Poland as opposed to in exile in London) was disbanded on 27 June 1945, bringing the Underground State to an end. The National Unity Council's closing demands for democracy and for the Red Army to leave Poland did not happen. The Provisional Government of National Unity took its place.

Stalin's promise for 'free and unfettered' elections seemed in doubt when sixteen leaders of the Polish Underground State were arrested and tried in March.

The Government-in-Exile continued to operate until the fall of communism and its last president, Ryszard Kaczorowski, would hand the presidential insignia and seal of office to Solidarity's leader, Lech Wałęsa, in 1990. Post-war research into the Polish Underground State had been restricted by the communists and historians could only eventually start telling the full story of resistance in Poland forty-five years after the war ended.

The Home Army

The Home Army or *Armia Krajowa* was formed when the Armed Struggle Union merged with most of the other underground organisations in February 1942. It was the military wing of the Underground State and followed directives issued by the London-based Government-in-Exile. The Home Army had three main tasks:

1. To carry out sabotage, intelligence and assassination missions against the Nazis.
2. To form and train units and collect arms and ammunition.
3. To prepare to revolt against the Wehrmacht when the Red Army advanced across Poland.

The Home Army headquarters had five sections: organisation, intelligence, training, logistics and communications. It also had two offices, one to look after finances and the other to produce and distribute propaganda. Two directorates organised resistance and special operations. The Home Army commander was supposed to report to the commander-in-chief of the London-based Government-in-Exile and the Warsaw-based Government Delegation, but he often acted independently if an opportunity presented itself.

The first commander was Stefan Rowecki (Spearhead), but he was arrested in Warsaw on 30 June 1943 after being betrayed by three traitors working for the Gestapo. He was questioned and tortured before being executed in August 1944. Tadeusz Komorowski was the commander who decided to launch Operation Tempest in the summer of 1944, but he would be captured at the end of the Warsaw Uprising in October 1944. He was held in a German prisoner-of-war camp and then had to emigrate to Britain at the end of the war to escape the NKVD. The final commander was Leopold Okulicki and he disbanded the Home Army in January 1945 because the Red Army were arresting and executing its soldiers. He was arrested by the NKVD as one of the 'Trial of the Sixteen' in the spring of 1945. He warned, 'Gestapo methods are child's play in comparison with the NKVD' before he was murdered in December 1946.

Command of the Home Army was initially divided into the Warsaw, Western, North-East and South-East regions, which were in turn split into sub-regions. It was reorganised along the same regional lines as the pre-war Polish Army in 1943, to cope with the large number of units. There was a rigid military hierarchy, from operational groups and divisions down to battalions and companies. The smallest unit was the platoon which typically had around forty active members with another twenty in reserve.

There were three types of Home Army soldier and they operated according to their local environment. Rural partisans lived in groups in the forests, attacking passing convoys or nearby military posts and depots. Urban partisans lived separately and met in secret to plan operations. Full-time members operated under false identities and codenames and often moved house every few days. Part-time members were occasionally called upon to participate in operations. They lived at home and had to live double lives so they would not put their family at risk.

The Home Army grew from 100,000 on formation to around 550,000 by the summer of 1944, making it Poland's main resistance movement. It was also the largest underground army in World War II and played a vital part in helping the Allies to fight the Germans. Spies collected information on all aspects of the German military and security services, providing nearly half of all the European-sourced intelligence reports which reached Britain. Information was provided on installations as diverse as the Vengeance Weapon testing sites (*Vergeltungswaffen* or V-2 rockets), the ghettos and the concentration camps.

Sabotage attacks and assassination missions were carried out by the Retaliation Union to begin with, the Fan units (*Wachlarz*) followed the Wehrmacht as it advanced into the Soviet Union during Operation Barbarossa. The two types of units merged their operations under the Diversion Directorate (*KeDyw*) at the start of 1943. They attacked arms factories, storage areas, refuelling depots and railway lines, and several German divisions had to be deployed to protect them.

The Home Army provided information about roundups and other police activities to try to protect Polish civilians. They tracked down and assassinated Nazi war criminals after subjecting them to trials in their underground courts. They also waged Operation N, a campaign of propaganda which involved distributing leaflets, putting up posters and painting graffiti.

Weapons and Equipment

The Home Army was always short of weapons and ammunition. They came from a variety of sources: a lot had been buried by Polish soldiers in September 1939 and were dug up when they were required (but some were too rusty to use); some were captured during raids on arms dumps or depots; some were taken from soldiers when they were mugged or executed; others were bought on the black market; and secret factories were set up to make copies of weapons.

Allied planes dropped around 600 tons of supplies to the Home Army, including cash and gold so more weapons and ammunition could be bought. More would have been delivered if the Soviets had allowed planes to use their airfields. A higher priority was placed on supporting the French resistance, not least because their drop zones were closer and easier to reach than the Home Army's.

Relations with Others

The Home Army was reluctant to recruit Jews into its ranks, but its Information and Propaganda Office opened a Jewish Affairs Section which supported the Jewish Relief Council (codenamed Żegota). There were attempts to get arms to the Jews in the Warsaw ghetto, and members tried to help during the uprising in the spring of 1943.

The Germans promised the Lithuanians the right to self-govern, so they helped track down Polish partisans around Wilno. The Home Army retaliated in the autumn 1943, targeting the Lithuanian Protection Teams, the Lithuanian Defence Force and the Lithuanian Secret Police. The violence spiralled, especially after the Home Army leaders refused to join Povilas Plechavičius's Lithuanian Detachment in their fight against the Soviets. The Germans encouraged the infighting and it culminated with the massacre of many civilians during the battle of Murowana Oszmianka in May 1944.

On 22 June 1943 Moscow instructed Soviet partisans to attack any Home Army units they could find. There were many fierce encounters and the Polish partisans often ended up hating their communist counterparts more than the German soldiers. Wehrmacht units occasionally donated arms and supplies to Home Army units to get them to do their work for them, but they always refused to collaborate with the Germans.

The End of the War

The Red Army advanced across Polish territory in 1944 and there was a truce with the Home Army to begin with. Partisan units staged uprisings to help the Soviets with their battles and they sometimes cooperated against the withdrawing Wehrmacht. However, Soviet commanders started arresting Home Army officers, conscripting suitable men into the Red Army, and deporting those deemed to be troublemakers to the Gulag.

General Okulicki eventually disbanded the Home Army on 19 January 1945 to avoid further confrontations with the Red Army. But the National Liberation Committee refused to take responsibility for ex-members, so the NKVD were kept busy disarming and interrogating them. Many refused to give up and they continued to fight the communist state long after the war was over. Both Moscow and the National Liberation Committee had them hunted down, arrested and often executed. They would become known as the 'Cursed Soldiers'.

Sabotage and the Diversion Directorate

The Diversion Directorate (the *Kierownictwo Dywersji* or *KeDyw*) was founded by Emil Fieldorf in January 1943, by merging the Fan units, the Retaliation Union and the Little Andrews. They continued to attack targets, and members were often trained by members of the Silent Unseen who had been taught in Britain.

Some KeDyw operatives stole or used bribes to acquire weapons and ammunition while some ran secret factories which assembled homemade versions. Others tracked down senior Nazi officers, looking to assassinate them, or scouted security and military organisations with a view to disrupting their work. Some units passed on their skills at military schools, some operated underground field hospitals.

The KeDyw started their work in the towns and cities, targeting military depots and arms factories. They also staged prison breaks and sabotage attempts on administration buildings. However, they had to move into the countryside when the Germans stepped up their security to avoid the many roundups. The saboteurs then concentrated on blowing up railways and road bridges to interfere with military movements.

The KeDyw units based around Warsaw moved into the city to take part in the uprising in August 1944. Jan Mazurkiewicz (codename Radosław) organised members into three battalions, called Sophie, Parasol and Broom, and they played an important part in the battle because they had weapons and experience. They began by seizing the Wola district, on the west side of the city, but were soon driven back into the Powązki Cemetery. They fought on in the city centre and old town until the end of the siege and many experienced fighters lost their lives.

Home Army Operations

The series of assassination attempts against senior German officials was called Operation Heads; a reference to the Death's Head symbol on the SS insignia. The Polish Underground held Special Courts which sentenced Nazi police officials and Gestapo officers who organised the round-ups and executions, and the labour office staff who controlled the deportations. Their aim was to make senior officials fear for their lives and the number of assassination attempts had risen from around twenty a month in 1942 to over one hundred by 1944.

SS–Obersturmführer Herbert Schultz and Gestapo officer SS–Rottenführer Ewald Lange were assassinated in May 1943 for torturing the Grey Ranks leader Jan Bytnar (codename Rudy) to death. Franz Bürkl and August Kretschmann, the commandants of Pawiak and Gęsiówka prisons in Warsaw, were killed in September. Three hits were made on 1 February 1944: SS and

Police Leader Franz Kutschera, Willi Lübbert of the labour office, and the intelligence agent Albrecht Eitner.

Kutschera was a target because he had increased the frequency of public executions and roundups across Warsaw when he took over in September 1943. He was spotted by Aleksander Kunicki (codename Rayski) as he travelled from his house to the nearby SS offices. Emil Fieldorf and Bronisław Pietraszewicz (code name Lot) were given the task of assassinating the hated officer. The first attempt on 28 January 1944 was aborted because Kutschera stayed at home, but the team killed him four days later; four of the assassination team lost their lives.

The following day 300 civilian hostages were executed and a 100 million złoty fine was imposed on the people of Warsaw, but Operation Heads continued. The Governor of the Warsaw district, Ludwig Fischer, escaped an attack, but the head of Warsaw's Security Service, Walter Stamm, was assassinated in May, and Karl Freudenthal, who had organised the deportation of the Jews from the Garwolin district, was killed in July. SS and Police Leader of Kraków Wilhelm Koppe was assassinated in the same month.

The Home Army targeted the border posts around the General Government on four occasions between August 1943 and February 1944, under the codenames Belt and Chain. One coup was the stealing of V2 rocket parts in the summer of 1944. Germany scientists had relocated their rocket launching site to Blizna in central Poland after the Royal Air Force bombed the Peenemünde site in northern German in August 1943. A Home Army agent reported a guarded train carrying a 'monstrous torpedo' in March 1944 and then Bletchley Park Code and Cipher School in England confirmed the location of the new site. Testing began in July 1944 but a crashed rocket was soon located and taken to the Home Army's laboratories in Warsaw to be analysed. Operation Bridge III (Operation Wildhorn III in British documents) transferred the parts from Poland, via Italy to London, where British scientists studied how to counter the terror weapon.

The Silent Unseen, 1943–45

British, Commonwealth and Polish pilots flew dozens of supply missions from Italy between August 1943 and July 1944. Many air drops delivered weapons, ammunition, cash and gold to the Silent Unseen. However, the long night flights over occupied Poland were dangerous and one in seven planes were shot down as they searched for their drop zones. Members helped train members of the KeDyw and they often joined them on operations. Nearly one hundred of the Silent Unseen took part in the Warsaw Uprising, in August and September 1944, but few survived.

Other Partisan Groups

The Peasant Battalions and Poland's Fighting Camp eventually joined the Home Army in the summer of 1944. However, partisan groups formed by those on the extremes of the political spectrum refused to join. Those from the left wing formed the People's Guard and then the People's Army while those from the right wing formed the Rampart Union and the National Armed Forces. It brought the number of partisans who were not affiliated to the Home Army to around 100,000.

The Workers Party formed the People's Guard in the German zone in January 1942. The communist partisan group refused to join the Home Army and it is thought that the Red Army and the NKVD helped it carry out sabotage and reprisal attacks. Full-time members found targets and then used part-time members to attack railway lines, blow up stations and derail trains. They also bombed offices, theatres and cafés used by the Germans.

Bolesław Mołojec was executed after being accused of the murder of his colleague Marceli Nowotko at the end of 1942, but the People's Guard went from strength to strength: it had 10,000 members by the end of 1943. They tried to stop the deportation of Poles from the Zamość region and helped the Jews during the Warsaw ghetto uprising.

The State National Council established the communist People's Army in January 1944 and General Michał Rola-Żymierski (codename Sea or Zawisa) took his orders from Moscow. The State National Council ordered the People's Guard to join it in July 1944, increasing membership to 25,000. Again, weapons, equipment and ammunition were acquired by various means; the Soviet Air Force dropped a considerable number. Rola-Żymierski was assisted by Franciszek Jóźwiak (codename Witold) and stories about his part in robberies and atrocities were suppressed after the war.

The People's Army claimed they carried out many operations against military targets, but their critics believed they carried out far less and that they often chose soft targets. Some partisans were also accused of fighting Home Army units and betraying their movements to the Gestapo. Even so, several hundred members took part in the Warsaw Uprising. The People's Army became part of the People's Army of Poland in July 1944 and it joined the First Polish Army a few months later.

The National Armed Forces

The Lizard Union and part of the National Military Organisation merged to form the National Armed Forces in September 1942 and membership had risen to around 70,000 when it split into two groups in March 1944. The moderates transferred to the Home Army but the right-wing members formed the Holy Cross Mountains Brigade (the mountains are in central Poland). They would attack the Germans, the Soviets and the Polish communist partisans. The Brigade withdrew ahead of the Red Army advance in January 1945, and the Germans allowed them to withdraw into the Protectorate of Bohemia and Moravia. Their final act of the war was to liberate prisoners from Flossenbürg concentration camp in Czechoslovakia. However, their fight was not over because the NKVD tracked down and arrested its members. The communists banned post-war research into the National Armed Forces, but members were finally rehabilitated by the Polish state in 1992.

Problems in South-East Poland

Many ethnic Ukrainians lived in the area that had once been south-east Poland and they resented the Poles because of discrimination before the war. The Ukrainian Nationalist Organisation wanted independence and the Ukrainian Insurgent Army started attacking Polish villages early in 1943. The Poles did what they could to defend their villages, with help from the Home Army, but thousands were massacred.

The Germans wanted to populate the Zamość region between Lublin and Lviv with ethnic Germans because it had fertile soil. They planned to remove over 100,000 people from 300 villages and replace them with 60,000 ethnic Germans. Originally Zamość was going to be renamed Himmler's City (*Himmlerstadt*) but the name was later changed to Plough City (*Pflugstadt*). The main deportations, codenamed Werewolf I and II, took place in the summer of 1943 and they were accompanied with a lot of violence. Villages were burnt down, people were shot, and children were kidnapped. The able ones were sent to Germany to work while the rest were sent to Warsaw, Lublin or a concentration camp. The Home Army, the Farmers Battalions, the People's Guard and Soviet partisans stopped most of the deportations over the winter of 1942.

The situation was complicated when the Ukrainian Insurgent Army started attacking the partisans and civilians at the beginning of 1944. More

Home Army units were formed when Operation Tempest began in August 1944 and they took control of many areas. The Germans tried to restore order with Operation Whirlwind, but they had to withdraw when the Red Army began attacking. Both the Polish and Ukrainian partisans turned on the Soviets as they advanced across the trouble area.

The movement of 31 million people across post-war Eastern Europe.

Chapter 16

We Saved You from the Nazis

Ethnic Cleansing and Polish Communities Abroad

The Cursed Soldiers

Stalin and the National Liberation Committee wanted to dismantle the Polish Underground State. The Home Army had tried to cooperate with the Red Army but that had only led to arrests, and the Soviets refused to assist the Poles during the Warsaw Uprising. The Home Army disbanded on 19 January 1945 so as not to jeopardise its members, and while many returned to civilian life, some continued to fight for Polish independence.

The Polish Committee of National Liberation refused to take responsibility for the ex-Home Army soldiers, so it was down to the NKVD to round up those referred to as the Cursed Soldiers. Around 60,000 had been arrested by May 1945, many after being promised an amnesty, and most were sent to the far flung territories of the Soviet Union.

Some of the Cursed Soldiers tried to free their comrades from prisons, others tried to assassinate NKVD officers and Public Security Ministry officials. All the inmates of the NKVD camp at Rembertów were rescued on 21 May 1945 before they could be deported to Siberia, but it was a rare success in the face of the powerful Red Army.

The NKVD and the new Polish Secret Police (the *Urzad Bezpieczenstwa* or UB) used deception, violence and interrogations to find thousands more. In June 1945, round-ups around Suwałki and Augustów in north-east Poland resulted in the arrest of 2,000 Cursed Soldiers. Around 1,400 were deported to Siberia and the rest disappeared in what became known as the 'Little Katyń' massacre.

The Freedom and Independence organisation was founded in September 1945 with the aim of stopping Soviet domination over Poland. Members were well-armed and they performed jailbreaks, identified collaborators and assassinated agents. They supplied arms and information to different partisan groups and made sure that the United Nations Security Council knew that the Polish referendum had been rigged in 1946. But the Polish Secret Police and the NKVD worked hard to infiltrate the organisation and the end came in the spring of 1947 when the authorities promised an amnesty. Most of the members came out of hiding and the leaders were arrested and executed, accused of plotting the overthrow of the People's Republic. The organisation never recovered, and it shut down in 1953.

The Polish People's Republic announced an amnesty for ex-Home Army members in the spring of 1947 and around 53,000 gave themselves up. Many were arrested because Colonel Julia Brystiger of the Ministry of Public Security called them terrorists. The Freedom and Sovereignty organisation had been set up to help Home Army soldiers integrate back into civilian life, but it lacked money and it too was disbanded in 1952. It was 1956 before 35,000 former Home Army soldiers were freed, having spent ten years in the Soviet Gulag system.

Ethnic Cleansing

Nazi Germany had spent five and a half years murdering and enslaving the Polish people, and the Soviets had spent seventeen months doing the same at the start of the war in the east of the country. The post-war change in Poland's borders left millions of people in the wrong country and the respective governments were well aware of the problems that minorities had caused in the past.

Both Poland and the Soviet Union wanted to ethnically cleanse their territories, resulting in the forced deportation of communities across Eastern Europe. Poles were moved out of Germany and the Kresy, Lithuanians, Byelorussians, Ukrainians and Germans were moved out of Poland. This is a record of the huge forced migration of over thirty million people in four years. While the narrative follows the deportations by ethnic groups, the mass movement of people was carried out simultaneously.

Moving Ethnic Germans from Poland to Germany

Both the Soviet and Polish governments wanted rid of all Germans from Polish territory. The Soviets wanted them removed for security reasons, the Poles wanted them out to end the ethnic violence. But they both saw it as revenge against the Germans.

The first wave of German expulsions came in January 1945 as a result of rumours and propaganda warning of massacres committed by the Red

Army as it advanced. The Nazi authorities refused to deport anyone because it would be seen as defeatist, but the stories were true because Soviet soldiers were committing robbery, rape and murder. Over four million ethnic Germans chose to flee: 100,000 people fled Łódź alone as the Red Army troops approached. Most who were fleeing were women, elderly or children and many would succumb to the winter weather during the long walk to Germany.

The authorities delayed the deportation of German civilians until the last moment and the roads were then filled with refugees; tens of thousands would die from the winter conditions or air attack. Around 250,000 women, the elderly and children were evacuated from the Baltic ports under Operation Hannibal, but there were disasters: 9,000 died when a Soviet submarine sank the *Wilhelm Gustloff* in January 1945 and thousands more died when American planes bombed Swinemünde harbour to stop the exodus. The Red Army halted along the Oder-Neisse river line in May 1945, occupying Germany's eastern territories. One million ethnic Germans had left in just a few weeks, many of them escaping the criminal gangs and groups of marauding Red Army soldiers roaming the area.

Moscow's Central Committee issued an order on 26 May 1945 ordering the rest of the Germans to leave the Oder-Neisse border area within one year. Polish police officers and Red Army soldiers were deployed to round them up and split them into those who could work and those who could not. The old and the weak were taken to railway stations and taken to Germany on slow moving wagons or open trucks.

Those fit enough to work were then marked out for abuse, by painting swastikas on their clothes or making them wear armbands marked *Niemiecki* (Polish for German). They were held in the abandoned concentration camps while their backgrounds were checked to see if they had worked for the Nazi Party. Serious perpetrators were tried as war criminals and executed while those accused of lesser crimes were imprisoned in the old concentration camps where they were subjected to violent attacks by the guards. The rest were put to work clearing rubble from the streets or building temporary homes in the war-damaged cities. If they survived long enough, they were then forced to walk across the border into Germany or Austria. Again, many died en route, and while figures vary, the accepted number of deaths is around 600,000.

But as tens of thousands of Germans moved west to avoid the dangers, equal numbers were heading east, back to their homes in what was now Polish territory. The Soviet and Polish authorities soon stopped the chaotic situation by closing the new border with Germany on 1 June 1945.

Those left behind then faced more detailed assessment, as the authorities investigated mixed marriages, those of mixed ethnicity and even those who had German-sounding names. They were particularly suspicious of those who had enrolled on the Volksdeutsche list at the beginning of the war. Some had done so to get preferential treatment, but many had joined because they feared for their lives. They were investigated and those who had willingly put their names down were deported. Those who had been forced to enrol could stay but they were also put to work clearing up war damage.

The remaining ethnic Germans faced food shortages, while a lack of policing left them at the mercy of criminal gangs and Red Army soldiers. Many Poles wanted to exact their revenge against the collaborators and Germans still living in their area and they were often attacked before they were sent to a labour camp and put to work.

Premier Josef Stalin, American President Harry Truman and British Prime Minister Clement Attlee discussed the ethnic cleansing of Poland at the Potsdam Conference in August 1945. Only this time it would be the deportment of ethnic Germans to the west. They also considered the relocation of millions of Poles because the Soviet Union wanted them out of the Kresy. It would involve the movement of millions of people of all ages across war-torn countries.

The Potsdam Agreement said that the transfer of Germans had to be carried out in an orderly and humane manner. The Soviet occupation forces and the Polish administration argued over how to carry out the deportations while the State Repatriation Office could do little to alleviate the plight of the refugees. The influx of over two million Polish settlers from the Kresy only added to the problems. The Germans became increasingly anxious to leave because they were being targeted by criminal gangs, Soviet soldiers, deserters and Poles returning from forced labour in Germany.

The transportation centres and internment camps became filled with people as the Americans and British questioned why so many refugees were being sent; the French even stopped accepting them. It left the homeless Germans at the mercy of ruthless guards and criminals until the problems were sorted out.

The transfers began early in 1946 but again many of the elderly and infirm refugees died in the harsh winter weather. They endured long waits at railway stations, prolonged journeys in cattle wagons and then more delays at processing centres as plans for an orderly deportation of 7.6 million people descended into chaos. But the refugees' troubles were just starting, because they were dumped in another war-torn area with just a few belongings. Eastern Germany was occupied by Soviet troops, violence and crime were rife, and the locals viewed the newcomers as a drain on the limited housing, food and work.

Exchanges Across the Eastern Border

The Poles had fought Lithuania, the Soviet Union and the Ukraine for the land east of the Curzon Line after the First World War. They called their new territories the Eastern Borderlands (*Kresy Wschodnie* or *Kresy* for short). Poland colonised the sparsely populated lands over the next twenty years but the Soviet Union always coveted the region. The post-war border had been set to the west of the Kresy at the Tehran Conference in November 1943 and the Polish Government-in-Exile complained that it had not been consulted. Poland was also forced to give the rich upper San River area and the Soviets began building coal mines in their new area as soon as the Poles had been deported.

The change in the border left over two million Poles inside the new Soviet Socialist States of Lithuania and Belarus. The Potsdam Conference had agreed that they should be moved to the German territory which had been given to Poland, in exchange for the Kresy. They would fill the vacuum created by the evacuation and deportation of hundreds of thousands of Germans from the area.

The Soviets wanted all the Polish intelligentsia out of the Lithuanian and Byelorussian areas, and while some were threatened with conscription into the Red Army, others were held in prison until they promised to leave. Many families quit because they did not want their children to be taught a Soviet curriculum in Ukrainian or Russian. Nearly one million had been deported by August 1946, but the Soviets had stopped thousands of peasants leaving because they needed them to work in the factories and on the land. Paperwork problems, threats and arrests made sure that only half of the 800,000 Poles who had registered to leave were allowed to go.

Refugees were only allowed to take what they could carry and they often had to wait a long time for the trains to take them west. Entire communities were moved together to the Recovered Territories and the Poles from Belorussia were taken to the north-west of Poland while those from Ukraine were moved to the south-west. Poland sent similar numbers of Byelorussians and Ukrainians east in return. The exchanges, codenamed Operation Vistula, would continue until 1951.

The largest exchange of people in the east was across the border with the new Ukrainian Socialist Soviet Republic. The Ukrainian Insurgent Army had been fighting the German Wehrmacht and the Polish Home Army in a brutal ethnic conflict since 1943. For example, the Ukrainians took the opportunity of the chaos at the end of the war to massacre around 50,000 Poles in the Volhynia district. The Poles fought back when possible, but the Soviet Union was determined to restore stability to the area again by deporting the troublemakers.

Moscow and Warsaw eventually acted following the assassination of the Polish communist General Karol Świerczewski on 28 March 1947. Around 140,000 Poles were deported under Operation West between May and July 1947 and they were given homes and financial help. At the same time the NKVD deported the families of Ukrainian Insurgent Army members to Kazakh and Siberia under Operation East to reduce ethnic tensions. Around 20,000 men were subjected to hard labour while 100,000 women and children had to make a life in the east. Another 32,000 were killed fighting the Red Army or were captured and executed by the NKVD.

The influx of tens of thousands of refugees into areas confiscated from Germany, which became known as the Recovered Territories, was again chaotic. Towns and cities had been devastated by five years of war and they faced many problems. The families only had what they carried, they had little money and they felt unsafe because of the lack of policing. They also felt abandoned because the Polish government did not invest in the Recovered Territories until they knew what its future was going to be.

Altogether around 31 million people left or were deported from one country to another across Central and Eastern Europe between 1944 and 1948. Around thirteen million were Germans who had fled the Red Army or had been evicted by the Soviet-backed Polish authorities. The rest were Poles moved out of the Kresy, and Lithuanians, Byelorussians and Ukrainians moved into their respective Soviet Socialist Republics. The death toll during the largest forced population movement is disputed but it is believed that over half a million people, most elderly or young, perished trying to escape in terrible weather conditions.

A Polish Enclave in Germany

Three million homeless Poles across Germany found themselves free at the end of the war. Some had been forced labourers, some had been imprisoned in concentration camps, others had been prisoners of war. They were now called Displaced Persons (DPs) and a future in a communist-controlled Poland looked bleak for some.

The Allies decided to create a Polish enclave in north-west Germany where they could stay until the situation settled down and they chose the town of Haren. The Polish I Corps evicted the population on 19 May 1945 and 4,000 Poles were moved in. The town was called Lwów until the Soviets asked for it to be changed and it was renamed Maczków in honour of General Stanisław Maczków, the commander of the 1st Polish Armoured Division.

The locals renamed all the streets after ones they remembered in Warsaw or after Polish military units. They published newspapers and opened a school and a cultural centre so people could share their experiences. The Polish troops left for Britain in the autumn of 1946 because their lives would be in jeopardy if they returned to a communist Poland. The civilians either followed them or decided to risk returning to a communist Poland over the next two years. The people of Haren were allowed back into their town at the end of 1948.

A Polish Community in Britain

Over 225,000 Polish servicemen and women were serving under the British armed forces by the end of the war. They had hoped to return home after the defeat of Nazi Germany, but events referred to as the 'Western Betrayal' meant that they could not or dared not. Roosevelt, Churchill and Stalin had agreed to hand over the Kresy to the Soviet Union during the November 1943 Yalta Conference and they had not consulted the Poles. Further discussions at the July 1945 Potsdam Conference meant that ethnic Poles were going to be deported from the area, in return for Lithuanians, Byelorussians and Ukrainians. The Soviet-backed government in Poland meant it was unwise for anyone who had served in the Free Forces of the West to return home. The lack of Soviet help during the 1944 Warsaw Uprising, the 'Trial of the Sixteen', and the arrest and execution of ex-members of the Home Army, were just a few signs that they would be risking their lives if they went home.

Churchill had met opposition when he had reported the Yalta decision to parliament, but he did set the foundation for what would become a thriving Polish community across Britain. He said, 'His Majesty's Government will never forget the debt they owe to the Polish troops... I earnestly hope it will be possible for them to have citizenship and freedom of the British Empire, if they so desire.'

The Polish Resettlement Corps was formed in May 1946 and recruiting started in the autumn; 115,000 eventually signed up, seventy per cent of those eligible to join. Veterans of the fighting in France, Belgium and Italy joined, airmen of the Polish Air Force, sailors from the Polish Navy and members of the Women's Auxiliary Air Force joined. A lot of released prisoners of war also became members.

Many initially lived around Swindon, close to their wartime base, or in one of the many Resettlement Corps camps, while they learnt English and a trade. Many brought their families over from Poland and while trade unions complained about the large number of Poles entering the labour market, the public ignored the negative publicity. The introduction of the Polish Resettlement Act, the nation's first mass immigration law, in 1947 silenced the opposition. The Polish Resettlement Corps would close down in 1949 after helping 150,000 Polish ex-soldiers and their families to settle in the United Kingdom.

Many Poles eventually settled in British cities, often choosing to live near Polish churches. Many were servicemen, some recuperating from wartime injuries, but there were also released prisoners of war and concentration camp survivors. They would be helped by the Church and a number of charities, in particular the Sue Ryder Foundation.

The outline of pre-war Poland compared with the outline of post-war Poland.

Chapter 17

Like Putting a Saddle on a Cow

Adapting to post-war communism, 1945 to 1953

Post-War Poland

Western Europe celebrated the end of the Second Word War on 8 May 1945 but Poland's problems were far from over, as it faced communist rule under which Warsaw would be dictated to by Moscow. The nation's post-war experience can be divided into two phases. The harshest period lasted from the end of World War II, in May 1945, to Stalin's death, in March 1953. There was then a gradual thawing of attitudes from Moscow, as Poland experienced a long journey towards the removal of Soviet influence and becoming, once again, a self-governing democracy.

The new borders discussed at the war conferences were implemented, moving Poland west as the Soviet Union was given the Kresy in return for Germany's eastern territories. After the problems with ethnic minorities before the war, both Poland and the Soviet Union wanted to move everyone inside the new borders. That included sending all Germans west, and all Lithuanians, Byelorussians and Ukrainians east. All Poles would be concentrated inside the new borders. Finally, the Polish communists worked to implement their policies across the nation, with Moscow's support.

Roosevelt, Stalin and Churchill had discussed the amount of reparations each country would have to pay, but nothing had been decided. Poland had fought on the Allied side and yet the Soviet Union expected it to pay reparations and took what they wanted when the war ended. They dismantled factories, hospitals and infrastructure from a country which had been terribly ravaged by war. Companies were taken over and their equipment was shipped to the East while others had to sell theirs at low prices. Some were even made to pay for the transport costs.

One in five Poles were dead after five and half years of conflict; the highest percentage of any nation in the war. Around three million Polish Jews had died in the ghettos or had been gassed in extermination camps while another three million Polish Christians had been shot, worked to death, starved or had been killed in one of the many battles across the country.

Over 13 million ethnic Germans would flee or had been deported during the two years after the war ended while 5 million Poles returned home to their ravaged country. Around 2.8 million Poles returned from forced labour camps across Nazi Germany while another 2 million were deported from the Kresy (the eastern part of pre-war Poland) which had been annexed by the Soviet Union. The remainder came from other parts of Europe.

Those who remained or moved into Poland now faced a difficult future because the towns and cities were in ruins (Warsaw had been systematically destroyed) and large parts of the transport system needed repairing. Families struggled to find homes and many were reduced to begging until they could find work. They had to rely on the black market to survive because the usual methods of distributing food were not in place yet. Many workers also had to run their own factories, in the absence of their owners, until the state stepped in.

Criminal gangs were commonplace, in the absence of an organised police force, and families also had to be wary of the Red Army soldiers billeted in their area. They believed Poland was a capitalist country and they stole or destroyed most of what they got their hands on. They treated the Poles with contempt and often committed violence, rape and murder during drunken rages. The authorities rarely took action against such excessive behaviour, making the people suspicious of the new regime.

The NKVD

The Soviet Army's Northern Group of Forces remained in Poland, but the Soviet Interior Ministry usually used the People's Commissariat for Internal Affairs to maintain public order. The organisation was often referred to as the NKVD because of the Russian spelling of its title, *Narodnyy Komissariat Vnutrennikh Del*. It used agents to spy on people and officers to arrest and question suspects, often using torture to get the answers they wanted. Many of their victims were then executed or faced many years in the Soviet prison system known as the General Directorate of Camps (*Glavnoye UpravleniyeLagerey*) or Gulag.

A school had started training students from Belarus and Ukraine back in 1940 in Smolensk, but it had to close when Operation Barbarossa was launched in June 1941. It reopened when the Red Army went over to the offensive at the end of 1942 and Polish candidates were recruited from the Polish soldiers of the Kosciuszko Division.

Around 2,500 graduates followed the Red Army into Poland in July 1944, where they organised the local police, recruited informers and identified potential enemies under the guidance of their Soviet advisors. Their chief role was to locate and engage the local Home Army and other partisan groups operating in their area. They had recruited over 20,000 members by the end of 1945.

Nikita Khrushchev cut back on NKVD investigations when he became First Secretary in 1953 and thousands of prisoners were freed or had their charges dropped, claiming there was a lack of evidence. Many who had charges hanging over them were too frightened to apply to have their names cleared.

Around six million Polish citizens had been questioned by the NKVD by the time the Soviet Army's Northern Group of Forces left Poland in 1956; around 300,000 had been arrested (some say the number was much higher) and 6,000 death sentences had been issued. Another 20,000 people had died in prison, many at the hands of their guards.

The Economy and Infrastructure

The government seized all land, houses and factories across Warsaw in October 1945; or rather they took ownership of the ruins. Families returned to what remained of their homes and made the best life they could in the face of many hardships. Government propaganda repeatedly told them that the Soviet Union was helping to rebuild their nation when in fact the Red Army was stripping factories and infrastructure and shipping everything east. A hatred for the West was also being drilled into the people with the help of Soviet-backed propaganda which said the Americans 'were rebuilding the neo-Nazi Wehrmacht and preparing it to invade Poland'.

Jozef Sigalin had opened the Capital Reconstruction Bureau back in February 1945, and Soviet and Polish architects had been discussing what sort of cities they wanted to see in the future. There was a lot of work to do after five years of war, and 85 per cent of Warsaw's buildings had been destroyed. But the Poles wanted their medieval cities back while the Soviets wanted modern designs with wide streets, large plazas and buildings made of concrete, glass and steel.

The modern Soviet plans were often thwarted by a struggling economy and poor planning but both types of architecture were pursued, resulting in a hybrid mixture of architecture. For example, Warsaw's huge Culture and Science Palace (which would be the tallest building in Europe for many years) was surrounded by mixture of old-style housing and modern apartments.

The government found it easy to nationalise all factories with over fifty employees in January 1946 because the owners were either dead or living in exile. Any new owners who complained about high quotas had their companies confiscated, while the workers often went on strike because they were being forced to work harder for less money.

The Polish government announced a Three-Year Plan to restore the country's economy in 1947, supported by a nationwide propaganda campaign. However, impossible targets were set and half of all the private firms closed because they struggled to abide by the strict government policies. The market became controlled by price regulations, high taxation, licensing and permits, and there were limitations on staff numbers and raw materials. Businesses often had to break the law or restructure their production methods to get around the rules. The enforced employment of peasants in industry created many problems.

Central government set wages in all state-owned factories but there were no overtime payments or incentives to encourage employees to work harder. It meant they worked slowly if they were given low quotas or produced poor quality items if they were too high. Employers who worked exceptionally hard were called 'Heroes of Labour' and were used to encourage others to increase their work rate.

The Soviets confiscated twenty per cent of Poland's agricultural land from landowners and gave it to peasants to run. Land reform was initially popular but sharing livestock and machinery under collectivisation was viewed with suspicion. Those who came from Poland's eastern territories were particularly cautious because they remembered the stories of the famines across the Soviet Union. They were right to be worried because the central government failed to distribute tools, seed and animals, so many families faced starvation.

Poland's economy struggled because central planning and a weak currency made it difficult to trade with other countries, particularly capitalist ones. The economy was soon out of control and there were many shortages, especially in foodstuffs, due to incompetent distribution. 'Privateers' filled the gap in the market by stealing items to sell on the black market. There was a lot of stealing from government warehouses because the nationalisation of industries created shortages, while smuggling was rife. Meanwhile postwar rationing meant that people often had to obtain food and essentials by bartering or bought luxuries from the black market. Despite the problems, a new economic Six-Year Plan was announced in 1950.

The Army and the Secret Police

The People's Army had formed in the Soviet Union with Polish and Red Army officers and ex-Polish Army soldiers. It had served in several campaigns during the advance across Poland, with mixed fortunes. The corps and divisions formed the basis of the post-war Polish Army, which was called the Armed Forces of the Republic of Poland. It was renamed the Armed Forces of the People's Republic of Poland in 1952.

The Polish Army was part of the Soviet Northern Group of Forces, commanded by Marshal Konstantin Rokossovsky. He would draft 200,000 Polish political agitators into labour battalions and they were put to work in mines and quarries. Many died or were injured in accidents while others were crippled by the harsh working conditions and lack of health and safety.

General Stanisław Radkiewicz established a secret police force to keep control of post-war Poland and they were run by the Ministry of Public Security (MBP) and its regional offices (UBPs) after December 1944. Jakub Berman of the Soviet Politburo made sure that the ministry spied on, controlled, infiltrated and shut down all anti-communist organisations. General Serov helped Berman while the Red Army and the NKVD provided backup for the Security Department officers (UB officers).

They used informants and spies to infiltrate public and local government departments and anyone suspected of anti-communist activities was interrogated in the old concentration camps. The Ministry took over the military's intelligence section in 1947 and its influence continued to grow as anti-communist paranoia increased. It was employing tens of thousands of people by the early 1950s and there was eventually one UB officer for every 800 citizens.

But the Ministry of Public Security's activities came under the spotlight after Lieutenant Colonel Józef Światło travelled to East Berlin in November 1953. He had gone there to discuss the assassination of the journalist Wanda Brońska who had worked for Polish Free Radio, but he took the opportunity to defect. Operation Spotlight then broadcast his experiences, revealing how the Ministry falsified evidence, used repression to control the masses, extracted confessions through torture and executed many prisoners. The exposé resulted in the number of investigations being reduced while half the Ministry staff were sacked or questioned about their activities.

The Ministry's activities were also divided. The Public Security Committee took control of the secret police, government security and the gathering of intelligence. Meanwhile the Internal Affairs Ministry took control of the local government departments, the citizen's militia and all other civil organisations. The Ministry of Internal Affairs took over all the activities in 1956 and the secret police were renamed the Security Service. Around 300,000 Polish citizens had been arrested by the Ministry and its successors over ten years. Many spent long spells in custody while over 6,000 had been executed.

Culture and Censorship

Soviet influence was imposed on Polish culture, starting in March 1949. The Ministry of Culture had Soviet films subtitled or dubbed and distributed to cinemas while Soviet books were translated into Polish for libraries and schools. New centres were opened to promote Russian culture while students were put on exchange visits to learn about life in Russia.

The regime also compiled a list of black-listed authors, journalists, publishing houses and newspapers. Around 1,600 books and journals were prohibited, and they were taken from libraries to be destroyed or held in restricted archives. However, the censor, Tomasz Strzyżewski, defected to Sweden with a bundle of classified documents in 1977 and published them as *The Black Book of Censorship*.

The Ministry of Culture wanted to replace decadent art with politically acceptable items. But while it was easy to close privately-owned galleries, the experts from the Fine Artists Union argued over what pieces should be displayed in the state-owned galleries.

The Church

The head of the Ministry's religious department, Julia Brystiger (nicknamed Bloody Luna), declared war on the Church at the end of 1947 when she said she wanted to rid Poland of the 'opiate of the masses'. Bolesław Piasecki headed the PAX Association, which often argued with the Catholic Church over policy, approving of the trials and imprisonment of priests. It would undermine support for the Church with the help of its publication *The Universal Word*. PAX was later given control of Caritas, the charity distributing foreign aid and running the orphanages and soup kitchens, and it was used to get public support for its views.

The secret police used informers to spy on church masses and priests were arrested, put on trial or banned from teaching. Church-run schools, hospitals and nursing homes were closed while Caritas was eventually shut down. Some priests ended up working with the Freedom and Democracy Fighters Union which helped ex-members of the Home Army.

Cardinal August Hlond died in 1948, and the new Primate of Poland, Cardinal Stefan Wyszyński, protested in private rather than in public, leading many to think he was cooperating with the authorities. Wyszynski eventually agreed that the clergy would work with the regime, but he was still arrested in September 1953.

The authorities' attitude towards religion is demonstrated by their reaction when the famous painting of the *Weeping Mother of God* in Lublin Cathedral was reported to be shedding real tears in July 1949. A news blackout was implemented but thousands still flocked to see the miracle and police had to stop crowds gathering around the cathedral. Cardinal Wyszyński was forced to announce that there was no miracle while the government reported that the moisture had been caused by humidity.

Education and Poland's Youth

The Polish government was faced with educating a generation of illiterate children who had received limited schooling over the past six years while the younger ones had had none. The new curriculum used Soviet text books, which justified communist ideals, until Polish versions were printed. Children's books explained the benefits of Marxism and the problems of capitalism through story-telling while the Stalin leader cult was promoted through the adventures of Soso, Stalin's nickname.

There was a shortage of trained teachers because so many had been executed by the Nazis or the Soviets at the start of the war. Many who escaped the round-ups had been killed while serving in the Home Army or had been arrested by the NKVD towards the end of the war. A programme called the 'Social Advance' encouraged workers and peasants to take up teaching, and while the initiative overcame the staff shortage, there was a lowering of standards.

Schools were an important part in the education of the working classes, so teachers were always under surveillance and they could be denounced by the school directors, by parents or by the students. The Ministry of

Education started a systematic assessment of all teaching staff in 1948, aiming to remove anyone deemed to be politically unacceptable.

Children received extra schooling if their parents were party activists, and authorities launched initiatives to improve the low level of literacy in 1951. Schools introduced military-themed activities including gymnastics, parades, marching and wargames, while summer camps gave the children extra experience.

The Youth Union vetted university admissions but the state pushed higher education for the masses and the number of students attending higher education multiplied. The authorities created new higher education establishments for pro-communist students, but many came from peasant backgrounds and were unable to complete the courses.

The Scouting and Guides Association reformed with 250,000 members, many of whom had fought in the Grey Ranks, in December 1944. There were a few political incidents but the authorities decided against banning the association because its members would go underground. Instead the secret police dismantled the Association from within, through a network of infiltrators and informants. The Youth Association was established in February 1948 to replace the Scouting and Guides Association. Members were vetted for political suitability and they attended meetings in their uniforms which had a green shirt and a red tie. Membership had risen to two million by the time it was once again called the Scouting and Guides Association.

The YMCA was reformed in 1945 and members began to distribute food, aid, clothes and books across Poland's devastated cities. They also provided education for young people and put on concerts, which were a welcome source of entertainment in the post-war ruins. However, the Education Ministry distrusted the organisation while the Fighting Youth Union was jealous of its popularity. It was eventually declared 'a tool of bourgeois fascism' and disbanded in 1949.

The rest of Poland's youth started protesting through graffiti or by shouting abuse at the security services and some were arrested for their actions. They started listening to rock and roll music in the early 1950s and followed western styles, buying hip clothing on the black market. The *'bikiniarze'*, as they were known, often fought communist members of the Youth Union, sometimes on the streets and sometimes on the dancefloor.

The borders and major cities of modern Poland.

Chapter 18

Because Freedom is Priceless

The struggle for democracy, 1953 to 1991

The New Course

Communism was so ingrained in many people that they mourned Stalin's death on 5 March 1953. The town of Katowice in south-west Poland was even renamed Stalinogród in his memory. Liberals started calling for a laxer Polish version of communism but the hard-line Secretary of the Polish United Workers Party, Boleslaw Bierut, rejected their appeals. The moderate Władysław Gomułka was put under house arrest before he could become their leader.

A big change came in December 1953 after the senior secret police officer Józef Światło defected to the west. His radio broadcasts described how Polish life was being dictated by Moscow and explained the underhand techniques used by the Ministry of Public Safety. As a result, Gomułka was set free and the nation's security services lowered their profile.

The signing of the Warsaw Pact in May 1955 may have brought the satellites closer to Moscow, but the party members heard Nikita Khrushchev denounce Stalin's purges at the 20th Party Congress in February 1956. Bierut died of mysterious circumstances shortly afterwards and was replaced by the moderate Edward Ochab. He had the head of the Polish courts and many senior UB personnel arrested while political prisoners were granted amnesty.

A 'World Peace and Friendship Festival' was organised as a youth propaganda event in the summer of 1955. Many foreigners attended the multi-cultural event which had music, art and debates. Many Polish teenagers learnt that anti-western propaganda was false, and they were soon holding demonstrations against the oppressive administration.

Poznań workers went on strike in December 1955 when they realised they had been underpaid after their quotas were raised without their knowledge. The government did nothing, so the strikers demonstrated at the International Trade Fair the following June. Prime Minister Józef Cyrankiewicz refused to talk to them, so they seized weapons from a military school and attacked government premises, including the Party headquarters, police stations and a radio jamming office.

The regime responded by deploying 10,000 soldiers and 400 tanks on the streets. Dozens of protesters were killed and hundreds more injured during three days of rioting. The demonstration was blamed on Western agents, but the hard-liners were secretly criticising the government's recent relaxed attitudes. The people accused the Soviet generals who had deployed the military for the bloodshed.

Polish Defence Minister Marshal Konstantin Rokossovsky and the communist Natolin Group asked Moscow for help, so President Nikita Khrushchev went to Warsaw on 19 October. He ordered Soviet troops to close in on Warsaw but an angry Gomułka responded by deploying army and interior ministry personnel around the capital. For the first time the international community took an interest in Polish affairs, as Gomułka told Khrushchev that he could maintain control in Poland if he was allowed. The government may have been pledging loyalty to the Soviet Union, but the people took to the streets in their thousands to protest at its interference.

Gomułka was appointed First Secretary and his aim was to create a socialist state which accommodated Polish values and culture. Khrushchev agreed and around 250,000 Poles were allowed to leave the Soviet Union and return home. Marshal Konstantin Rokossovsky was recalled to Moscow, all the Russian officers had to leave the Polish Army, and the Soviet Union started to withdraw the Red Army from Polish soil. Cardinal Wyszyński was released from prison and the rights of the Church were restored in return for its support.

A new crisis hit the Soviet Union on 30 October 1956 when Budapest declared democracy. The Red Army invaded five days later and the world's attention turned to Hungary. Meanwhile the changes across Poland continued apace. The Stalinists were removed from the government, collectives were stopped and factory bosses were sacked. New associations were formed and new newspapers appeared, all supporting the regime.

There were more strikes but they continued to be denounced and Gomułka cracked down on them when he was re-elected in 1957. General Mieczysław took over the security services in 1959, and while they started harassing the church again, it became stronger as people sought solace from their faith.

Relations with the west were increasing through radio, travel and trade but the people were discovering that Poland's contribution to the war was being dismissed while its connections with communism were viewed with suspicion. They also learnt that the nation was being accused of anti-Semitism and even collaborating in the Jewish Holocaust. Poland needed to reinvent itself but there were difficult times ahead.

The Church sent letters to Germany in 1966 calling for reconciliation as it prepared to celebrate 1,000 years of Christianity in Poland. However, the Minister of the Interior, General Mieczysław Moczar, accused it of undermining the state. Then the Soviet Union supported the Arabs in the Six Day War in 1967 while Poland supported the Israelis because so many had Polish ancestry.

Another crisis came when Adam Mickiewicz's drama *Forefathers' Eve*, a story about Polish independence during the eighteenth century, was banned. Students demonstrated across Warsaw and there was violence when the Volunteer Reserve Militia attacked them. Thousands were arrested and many more expelled, resulting in more demonstrations across the country. Gomułka was once again forced to ask Moscow for help against what he called a conspiracy while Moczar blamed the disturbances on the Jewish community. Hundreds were sacked from their government and party jobs, while 15,000 Jews emigrated to escape harassment.

The Polish Army was always on standby ready to deal with social unrest. However, it was under Soviet control and 26,000 Polish troops had to take part in Operation Danube, the Warsaw Pact's invasion of Czechoslovakia in August 1968.

The Polish economy continued to struggle under the restraints of decentralisation and while costs rose, wages and living standards fell. Poor harvests in 1969 and 1970 resulted in food shortages and the government responded by increasing food prices by thirty per cent in December 1970 rather than import any. So the Gdańsk shipyard workers went on strike and marched on the Party headquarters to protest. Shots were fired and the building was burnt down, resulting in more strikes and protests in nearby Gdynia and Szczecin. The government deployed 27,000 troops supported by tanks to seal off the unruly areas and quell the violence.

Over forty were killed and one thousand were injured in violent confrontations while another 3,200 were arrested. First Secretary Gomułka suffered a stroke, and his replacement, Edward Gierek, took immediate action. Food prices were lowered, ending the strikes, while raw materials were promised to other countries in return for huge loans. The investments allowed work to start on housing and infrastructure projects while investments in factories resulted in a rise in production. Gierek kept food prices stable and living standards increased as the shortages disappeared.

Poland's future may have looked bright but managers were now running the country and they often held the workers and peasants in contempt. Many were incompetent and construction projects cost too much and took too long to finish. Factories were producing more goods, but they were often of sub-standard quality and could not be sold abroad.

A world recession damaged Poland's fragile economy beyond repair and Gierek had to raise food prices by sixty per cent in June 1976. There was another strike and the Citizens' Militia had arrested many before the government backed down and reduced prices. The usual economic problems were being increased because of the widespread corruption carried out by managers who had little faith in socialism. The problem was that the Polish workforce was being employed to turn foreign loans (often American dollars) into goods which could only be sold to the Soviet Union for roubles. So the country was borrowing a strong currency and converting it into a weak one.

Young Poles were turning against socialism and those who worked in the west were angry about the Soviet Union's control over their country when they returned home. Children of ex-pats were also visiting Poland, bringing news of what lay beyond the Iron Curtain. So there was a public outcry when Moscow called upon Warsaw to change the constitution, confirming the country's commitment to socialism and the Soviet Union.

The August 1975 Helsinki Accords called on all the signatory countries to respect the rights of their people. They had been ignored and abused during the recent strikes, so the Workers' Defence Committee was established in September 1976 to make sure they were protected in the future. Committee members offered legal advice, followed trials, paid fines and supported the families of those arrested. Irregularities and abuses could now be reported to Helsinki and they would then be reported by the media. The new accords meant that the Polish government had to tread warily and while it could not arrest Committee members, it still had them followed and harassed.

The date 16 October 1978 was a proud day for Poland because the Archbishop of Kraków, Karol Wojtyła, was elected Pope John Paul II. He had decided to join the priesthood back in October 1942 and he experienced hardships and danger as he completed his training in secret in Nazi-occupied Poland. The Pope's visit to his home nation in June 1979 saw hundreds of thousands of people hear him talk about respect and dignity at one of the open-air masses. The militia had to stand back as he told people never to give up or lose hope. The Pope's words were not forgotten and his visit would help to set Poland on a course to democracy.

Another world recession forced Gierek to increase food prices in July 1980 and the inevitable unrest followed. Only this time, workers locked themselves inside the Gdańsk shipyard on 14 August, protesting at the dismissal of their colleague Anna Walentynowicz. At their head was another sacked colleague, Lech Wałęsa. The workers of Szczecin also locked themselves inside their dockyard, so the soldiers and tanks could not get at them.

News of the sit-ins were broadcast around the world and a powerless Gierek offered to resign on 28 August. Instead an agreement guaranteeing free trade unions, freedom of information and civil rights was signed three days later. It looked as though the revolution against the authoritarian proletariat had resulted in a fair deal for the Polish workers.

On 17 September all the unions merged into the Independent Self-Governing Trade Union Solidarity. The logic was that it would be harder to infiltrate a large organisation with the resources to represent three million members. Lech Wałęsa was its leader and it would be known as *Solidarność* across Poland and as 'Solidarity' across the rest of the world. Its two main principles were to implement true socialism and to improve the lives of its members.

Stanisław Kania took over when Gierek had a heart attack and Moscow immediately put him under pressure to restore the situation. As Solidarity's numbers soared, he responded by preparing for martial law. The borders with Germany and Czechoslovakia were closed while the Soviet press agency, TASS, announced that the Red Army would be conducting military manoeuvres in Poland. Kania and his cabinet eventually flew to Moscow in December to ask for help on how to curb the surge in people power. They reported that Poland was facing economic disaster because it had run up huge foreign debts and could not borrow any more to pay for the upkeep of essential services. It was also unable to invest in its aging industries and they were pumping out masses of pollutants as they struggled to meet quotas.

The government could no longer keep taboo subjects, like Poland's independence, the Home Army, the Katyń massacre and the Warsaw Uprising, out of the media, while books, articles and films were appearing on these sensitive subjects. Prices started to rise again in 1981 and people were having to buy dollars from foreign currency shops so they could shop on the black market. It was too much for many and they headed to the west to look for work.

Solidarity kept calling for political and economic changes to improve the lives of the Polish workers and peasants. But the government kept delaying promised changes to trade union law while the Citizens' Militia Motorized Reserves (ZOMO for short) caused trouble at trade union meetings. Solidarity then threatened more strikes at the end of March, so Soviet military manoeuvres were televised as a veiled threat. Moscow was telling Warsaw to act and while it was prepared to implement martial law, the new American President, Ronald Reagan, told General Secretary Leonid Brezhnev to back down.

The summer of 1981 proved two important facts: the United Workers Party was divided, and Solidarity was united. The Soviet fleet held manoeuvres off Poland's coast while the trade union leaders discussed forming a political party and called for an election at its first National Congress in Gdańsk. Solidarity also called for the rest of the Soviet satellite states to follow their lead. Despite the rebellious behaviour, the Soviet Union was unable to do anything more than denounce what was happening in Poland. President Reagan was supporting Poland and the Soviet economy relied heavily on American trade and loans. Its army was also embroiled in an unpopular and difficult war in Afghanistan. The combination of factors made it unwise to do anything.

Stanisław Kania resigned in October 1981 and the new hard-line president, General Wojciech Jaruzelski, wasted no time in taking control of Poland. The country's telephone system was shut down late on 12 December, while the police arrested 5,000 Solidarity members, including all its leaders. Radio and television announced that a Military Council of National Salvation had been formed and martial law was in place the following morning. Troops and tanks deployed on the streets, while the ZOMO guarded the mines, factories and railways. There were strikes and sit-ins across the country and many ended in violence as workers confronted the paramilitaries. There were many more arrests over the winter as the people faced curfews and restrictions to travel. There were frequent confrontations and a wave of strikes and demonstrations on 3 May 1982, resulted in hundreds being injured and another 5,000 arrested.

Martial law was suspended in December 1982 and finally lifted in June 1983, but few were interested in joining a state-controlled trade union or the Patriotic Movement for National Regeneration. The Solidarity leaders had been released and they resumed spreading their message via the radio and newspapers, despite harassment from the security forces. The Church also started holding and supporting cultural events, with the help of overseas donations.

Meanwhile the government was facing continuing difficulties as inflation spiralled in the face of western economic sanctions, resulting in the devaluation of the złoty. The government were employing more people in the security forces than ever before, and the tyranny increased. Many people emigrated, while the suicide rate rose in the face of the increasing police presence and food shortages.

The end of martial law coincided with a second visit by Pope John Paul II, only weeks after a failed assassination attempt on his life. He met the banned union leader Lech Wałęsa and called upon a million strong crowd waving Solidarity flags to fight for trade union rights. The security forces countered by increasing investigations against the Church and even falsely claimed the Pope had fathered an illegitimate child.

General Jaruzelski had always tried to appease Moscow, but the appointment of Mikhail Gorbachev as General Secretary of the Communist Party in March 1985 changed everything. He introduced 'glasnost' and 'perestroika', which meant openness in government activities and political reform. Jaruzelski had been keeping order in Poland through a Military Council of National Salvation since 1981 and the Soviet Union's softer stance undermined his position, especially as the economy was failing under the weight of foreign debt.

Pope John Paul II returned to his home country in 1987, where he was again greeted by huge crowds waving Solidarity placards. Jaruzelski still refused to talk to Wałęsa but he had to form a Consultative Council in 1987 when a referendum rejected a new plan to restart the economy. Wałęsa countered by setting up an Interim Council. Austerity measures resulted in more strikes and violence in February 1988 and the new prime minister, General Czesław Kiszczak, eventually met Wałęsa on 31 August 1989.

The situation across Eastern Europe took a dramatic turn when the Berlin Wall came down on 9 November. It was the end of Soviet rule across Eastern Europe, as the East German, Czechoslovakian and Romanian regimes were overthrown one-by-one. Poland, however, stuck with its interim government and continued the existing reforms.

Both Solidarity and the Church had their legal statuses reinstated during 'Round Table' discussions which lasted from 6 February to 5 April 1990. More importantly, the presidential office and the bicameral parliaments were restored, so elections could be held; or rather interim elections, because two out of three seats in the Sejm would be reserved for the communist Polish United Workers' Party. The promise was that the 1993 elections would be entirely free.

Solidarity agreed to the restrictions and it won all but one of the one hundred seats in the Senate and all but one of the available seats in the Sejm. Many of their candidates failed to get the minimum number of votes to enter the second round. Even General Kiszczak had failed to get enough. Wałęsa agreed some candidates could take part in the second round of voting but Solidarity's victory was complete. However, its leaders were wary about what to do next because of the low turnout, so Jaruzelski suggested forming a coalition government. He was appointed president to reassure Moscow that Poland was still committed to the Warsaw Pact.

Prime Minister Tadeusz Mazowiecki named his ministers on 12 September and he included five communists in his cabinet to calm the Soviet Union's attitude towards Poland. The new government set about restoring a free market economy, improving the employment situation and opening foreign policy dialogues. It also amended the constitution, established an open local government and set up a state police force to replace the paramilitary Citizens Militia.

Poland's Communist Party disbanded at the end of the year, but its members immediately formed the Social-Democrat Party. Prime Minister Mazowiecki was also concerned that there were many former communists serving in the judiciary, the media, the army and the police; his Ministers of Defence and Interior were also former communists. The only way to secure their support was to draw a line under the nation's communist past; a bitter blow for the many who had suffered during fifty years of communist rule.

The end of Soviet rule prompted the masses to call for immediate free elections and two new political parties were formed to challenge Mazowiecki's government. There was the Confederation for an Independent Poland led by Leszek Moczulski and the Christian National Union led by Wiesław Chrzanowski. In May 1990 calls for immediate elections by the twins Jarosław and Lech Kaczyński at the Bureau of National Security worked.

Jaruzelski stood down, but Mazowiecki decided to challenge Wałęsa and the presidential pre-election discussions were dominated by unpleasant personal attacks. The Solidarity leader won and he was handed the pre-war presidential insignia and seal of office on 22 December 1990. They had been in London for fifty years and the President in Exile, Ryszard Kaczorowski, had travelled to Poland to symbolically recognise the continuity of his government with the new Third Republic.

Arguments over technicalities delayed the elections until 27 October 1991 but over one hundred parties would be represented. The result was inconclusive, but a centre-right coalition led by Jan Olszewski had been formed before the end of the year. There would be many unpleasant issues to solve from Poland's past and difficult problems to confront about the nation's future. But after more than fifty years of Nazi and Communist oppression, Poland was once again a free, democratic state.

Bibliography

The Eagle Unbowed: Poland and the Poles in the Second World War, Halik Kochanski, Penguin, 2013

Poland: A History, Adam Zamoyski, William Collins, 2015

Warsaw 1944: Hitler, Himmler and the Crushing of a City, Alexandra Richie, William Collins, 2014

Rising '44: The Battle for Warsaw, Norman Davies, Pan 2018

KL: A History of the Nazi Concentration Camps, Nikolaus Wachsmann, Abacus 2016

The Holocaust: A New History, Laurence Rees, Penguin, 2017

Masters of Death: SS-Einsatzgruppen and the Holocaust, Richard Rhodes, Vintage, 2003

Schindler's Krakow: The City Under the Nazis, Andrew Rawson, Pen and Sword 2015

Warsaw 1920: Lenin's Failed Conquest of Europe, by Adam Zamoyski, William Collins 2014

White Eagle, Red Star: The Polish-Soviet War 1919-20, Norman Davies, Pimlico, 2003

Trail of Hope: The Anders' Army, An Odyssey Across Three Continents, Norman Davies, Osprey 2015

No Greater Ally: The Untold Story of Poland's Forces in WWII, Kenneth K. Koskodan, Osprey 2011

The Forgotten Few: The Polish Air Force in World War II, Adam Zamoyski, Pen and Sword 2009

For Your Freedom and Ours: The Kosciuszko Squadron, Lynne Oleson, Arrow 2004

303 Squadron: The Legendary Battle of Britain Fighter Squadron, Arkady Fiedler, Aquila Polonica 2010

Museums

The Polish Institute and Sikorski Museum in London contains many artefacts and documents donated by Poles who could not return to their homeland after the war.sikorskimuseum.co.uk/

The following list gives links to the main museums across Poland relating to World War II and the Holocaust. Many city and town museums will have sections relating to this period:

Warsaw

Warsaw Uprising Museum	1944.pl/en
Polin, the Museum of Poland's Jews	polin.pl/en
Polish Army Museum, Warsaw	muzeumwp.pl/?language=EN
Katyń Museum	Part of the Polish Army Museum, Warsaw
Pawiak Prison Museum, Warsaw	museumofpawiakprison.tumblr.com/

Kraków

Home Army Museum	muzeum-ak.pl/english/
The Galician Jewish Museum	galiciajewishmuseum.org/en
Schindler's Factory Museum	mhk.pl/branches/oskar-schindlers-factory
Auschwitz Museum, Oswiecim	auschwitz.org/en/

Gdańsk

War Museum	muzeum1939.pl/en/home

Holocaust Related Museums

Majdenek Camp Museum, Lublin	majdanek.eu/en
Stutthof Camp Museum	stutthof.org/english
Chełmno Camp Museum	chelmno-muzeum.eu/en/
Treblinka Camp Museum (in Polish)	treblinka-muzeum.eu/
Sobibór Camp Museum	sobibor-memorial.eu/en
Bełżec Camp Museum	belzec.eu/en

Italy

Polish II Corps Museum	fondazionemm2c.org/en/

Memorials

This is a limited list of the main Polish memorials around the world:

Poland

Tomb of the Unknown Soldier: Plac Marszalka Jozefa Pilsudskiego, Warsaw

Monument to the Fallen and Murdered in the East: Muranowska, Warsaw, Poland

Monument to the Warsaw Uprising Fighters: Krasinski Square, Warsaw, Poland

Monument to the Ghetto Heroes: ul. Zamenhofa 11, Warsaw

Child Fighters Memorial: Podwale, Old Town, Warsaw

Female Couriers of the Home Army, Parkowa, Józefów

Monument to the Heroes of Warsaw: Nowy Przejazd, Warsaw, Poland

Josef Pilsudski Monument: Lazienki Park, Warsaw

Polish First Army Memorial, ul. Generala Wladyslawa Andersa, Warsaw

1st Infantry Division, Wybrzeze Szczecinskie, Warsaw

Enigma Codebreakers memorial, ul. Św. Marcin, Poznań

Marian Rejewski, code breaker, memorial, Gdanska, Bydgoszcz

Mila 18, Jews who took their lives rather than surrender: Junction of Mila and Dubois, Warsaw

Polish Underground State and Home Army: Wiejska Street and Jana Matejki Street, Warsaw

Polish Airmen Memorial, Mokotów Park, Warsaw

Kotwica Memorial (Anchor Memorial): Warsaw Uprising Hill, south-east Warsaw

Wojtek the Bear Memorial, Jordan Park, Kraków

Westerplatte Memorial, Gdańsk

The holocaust sites, Treblinka, Sobibór, Bełżec, Majdanek, Chełmno and Auschwitz, have memorials

Plasnow Camp Memorial, Kraków

Martial Law Memorial, Pilsudskiego and Swidnicka, Wrocław

United Kingdom

Polish Code Breakers memorial, Bletchley Park Museum, United Kingdom

Polish Armed Forces Memorial, National Memorial Arboretum, Lichfield, Staffordshire

Polish Air Force Memorial, Northholt, London

RAF Chailey Memorial to Polish Airmen, Plumpton
Wojtek the Bear Memorial, Princes Street Gardens, Edinburgh
Katyń Memorial, Cannock Chase
Katyń Memorial, Gunnersbury, London

America

Katyń Memorial, Jersey City, New Jersey

Canada

Katyń Memorial, Toronto

Russia

Katyń Memorial, Smolensk

Italy

The Polish Cemetery and Memorial at Monte Cassino

Israel

Monument to Jewish Military Casualties in Polish Armies, Mount Herzl
Jerusalem

Index